For Dot Jackson, who loves the Carolinas and their people as I do.

Acknowledgements

All but one of the pieces in this book originally appeared, in slightly different form, in the *Greensboro Daily News* or the *Charlotte Observer* and are used with permission. Those dated prior to April, 1977, appeared in the *Greensboro Daily News*, those afterward in the *Charlotte Observer*. The story on Luemer and Della Plumley appeared in *Southern Changes* magazine. The stories on Paula Sandburg, Henry Shirtz, Wimpy Lassiter and Carbine Williams also appeared in the *Atlanta Journal-Constitution Sunday Magazine*.

Contents

Introduction

It was only economics that kept me from being born a Carolinian. Years before, my mother's father had taken his family from the North Carolina foothills to Danville, Virginia, just over the state line, so that he might find work in the cotton mills. As a young man, my own father left the hills of Surry County, North Carolina, and made his way to Danville seeking work. There he met my mother and there I was born in the summer of 1941.

Soon after my birth, my father took my mother and me back to Surry County, to his father's small, red-dirt tobacco farm near Dobson, the county seat. We lived there for only a few months before moving to Thomasville, in the populous Piedmont, where my father got a job in a hosiery mill. There I grew up.

I always have thought of myself as a Carolinian, and the few times I have been away from the Carolinas for extended periods, I have longed to be back. Here I am comfortable. Here I am home.

Everything considered, I have been a very lucky man. Not only was I fortunate enough to grow up in what is, without doubt, one of the most beautiful and interesting areas of the country; but for the past 12 years, first as a reporter and columnist for the *Greensboro Daily News*, later as a columnist for the *Charlotte Observer*, I have had the incredible good luck to be paid to wander about this place I love, meeting people and writing about them. I have met hundreds of people in this work, and I always have been received with warmth and openness, with graciousness and generosity, traits common to Carolinians. They have made my job a pleasure as well as an education.

This book is about some of those people. They are a diverse group, as diverse as the Carolinas themselves. The one thing they all have in common is that they are, either by birth or choice, Carolinians. Most are North Carolinians. I do not mean to slight South Carolinians — or South Carolina — in including so few of them here. It is just that I have spent more time in my own state.

A few of the people you will meet here are so widely known that their names may be familiar. The great majority have led lives untouched by fame, and I'm sure they all would consider themselves quite ordinary people, although all are in some way extraordinary. It is my hope that these brief glimpses into their lives will capture some of the unique character of the Carolinas.

I have broken this book into three sections representing the three distinct geographic regions of the Carolinas. I did this for more than simple convenience. The lives and character of many of the people in this book were formed by the land on which they lived: by the vast waters and rich, flat farmlands of the coast, by the small towns and cities of the Piedmont, the rugged and isolated reaches of the mountains.

The land no longer has such a powerful effect on Carolinians. Industrialization, rapid transportation, instant communication and the population growth and devastation of the land and waters that have come with it have changed all that. It is important that the influence of the land on people's lives and character be preserved, if only in a book.

June, 1980
Asheboro, North Carolina

The Coast

ZSCHIESCHE

Survivors of a Dying Village

Three mornings a week — Mondays, Wednesdays and Fridays — Lum Gaskill climbs into his blue pickup truck and drives around the edge of Silver Lake Harbor to the post office in the island village of Ocracoke. He usually arrives by 8:30 and within a few minutes he has stuffed a handful of mail into a leather satchel and headed back to the harbor's end where he keeps moored a fishing boat and several skiffs.

This is Monday. In the tiny, weatherworn shack near the middle of a dock he dons waders and wetwear. He straps the satchel around his shoulder and wades into the shallow water, sending thousands of silver fingerlings, which have been swarming vengefully over the carcasses of two sharks, skittering in quick flashes to safety.

He lifts the anchor slowly, checks the small outboard motor on one of his skiffs and swings the boat around. He stashes the satchel under the bow so it won't get wet, climbs aboard, starts the motor sputtering, eases out of the harbor and heads toward the shoals of Ocracoke Inlet. It is seven miles to Portsmouth.

For the people of Portsmouth — the first and once the largest town on the Outer Banks, North Carolina's chain of fragile barrier islands — Lum Gaskill is the sole contact with the rest of the world.

Portsmouth Island was settled in the early 1700s. A charter for a town at the northern end of the island was granted in 1753. The town became the major port on the North Carolina coast.

By 1850, the population of Portsmouth was 500. After the Civil War, the town became a resort for the rich. But by then other ports, other inlets had opened and Portsmouth had begun its decline. Devastating hurricanes washed away the town's wharves and warehouses, but as recently as 1939 its population was still more than 100. By 1955, it had fallen to 18. Now it is five.

Gaskills were among the first settlers of Ocracoke and Portsmouth. Lum Gaskill, like his forebears, is a man of the sea. He is 55, a big, ruddy-faced man who speaks with the brogue peculiar to Outer Bankers. He spent 21 years in the Coast Guard. Now he rents cottages to tourists, fishes, and carries the mail to Portsmouth.

On this day, there are in his satchel four letters, two postcards

10

and a catalog. The water is choppy and the boat slaps the water, sending salt spray arcing back into Gaskill's face as he talks.

Fifty years ago, he says, the tavern at Portsmouth was still open. It was the first business in the town and the roughest. "You could buy whiskey by the barrel or by the bottle, any way you wanted it."

He remembers when there were still four grocery stores in town. The last closed 12 years earlier. It has been only seven years since the post office closed after more than 120 years of operation.

The old Coast Guard station and the white church steeple are the town landmarks. They can be seen, snuggled in the trees, all the way across the inlet. The Coast Guard moved out in 1938, returned during World War II, left again at war's end. The church, pastorless, remains open.

As the skiff nears land, Gaskill points to a grayed, broken-down building half hidden in vegetation. "That house is 200 years old," he says, "built of deck plank and pegs . . ."

He steers the boat toward a grassy bank jutting into the sound, moors it in shallow water, straps on his satchel, wades ashore and begins the short trek into town.

Modern conveniences end at Ocracoke. Portsmouth has no telephones, no electricity, no running water. Drinking water comes from the clouds, stored in cisterns. Light comes from kerosene lanterns and food is cooked on kerosene stoves.

The streets of Portsmouth are grassy trails almost lost in the tangle of woods and undergrowth that strangle most of the abandoned and decaying houses, some of them more than 150 years old. A few of the houses, maybe 10, have been rescued to be used as hunting and fishing lodges by wealthy mainlanders. The town has been trying vainly to beat back the wilderness. The clearings are few now.

The abandoned post office occupies the first clearing as you enter town from the northwest. It is small and white and a window has been broken. An old Jeep hulk is parked inside. But a hand-lettered sign over the door still proclaims this the post office and Portsmouth a town. The sign has been recently painted, Lum Gaskill points out.

The church is the center of town. It is a short distance up the trail from the post office through a marsh. A white heron, startled by Gaskill's approach takes gracefully to the air from the marsh.

The church has been well-tended. The door is held shut by two latches to keep the wind from banging it. Inside, it can be seen by

11

the way the walls lean that the building has survived many buffetings by wind and water. The altar is adorned with plastic flowers and to one side sits an ancient foot-powered organ. A collection plate and small guest book lie on a table before the pulpit. The table holds two neatly lettered signs: "Visitors, the permanent residents of Portsmouth welcome your contributions. All money will be used for the repair and maintenance of this church. Thank you." And, "Please do not put mosquito repellant bottles or cans on seats. It damages the varnish. Thank you." The collection plate contains four one-dollar bills and five pennies. The guest register, started four years earlier, is only half-filled.

The church is seldom used now, but a few months earlier a doctor and his bride-to-be from across the sound had chosen the church for the site of their wedding. It was the first wedding in the church in 51 years and Portsmouth's five residents are still talking about it.

There are two houses beside the church, one large, one small, both painted yellow, both neat and well cared for, with manicured lawns and picket fences. A small sign on the fence says canned soft drinks are available inside for 25¢. Mrs. Lillian Babb, age 73, lives in the big house with her daughter, Marion. Mrs. Babb's sister, Miss Eleanor Dixon, 65, lives in the small house. They have lived all their lives in Portsmouth.

Henry Piggot, 74, lives nearby in a little pink house by the swash. He is a thin, hollow-cheeked black man, one of the few blacks to live on the Outer Banks. He was born in Portsmouth. The fifth resident, Fred Cannon, a fisherman, lives two miles farther south. He is not a native. He came five years earlier from the mainland because he likes the isolation offered by the island. People in Ocracoke call him "the hermit."

On this morning, Mrs. Babb and her daughter are away in Morehead City to the southwest. They have gone to see a doctor and visit relatives. Because this is the day Lum Gaskill comes, the rest of Portsmouth's population is gathered in Miss Dixon's kitchen, which is, in the old style, separate from the house.

Lum Gaskill is more than just the mailman. He also brings supplies when they are needed, runs errands, and equally important, is somebody to talk with about what is happening in the world beyond the inlet.

Gaskill sprawls in a chair across the oilcloth-covered table from Henry Piggot. Fred Cannon sits by the wall. Miss Dixon busies herself around the small kitchen. The talk is of local news, politics and fishing.

Miss Dixon, a curly-haired, sad-faced woman, is hard of hearing and does not enter the conservation other than to ask if she has any mail. Cannon, whose face is leathery and deeply lined, keeps on his waders and fishing hat and listens quietly. Piggot and Gaskill do all the talking.

Henry Piggot lived with his two sisters until both died within a few months of each other about six years earlier. He has fished the whole coast, and for 15 years he carried the mail in Portsmouth. He was away from Portsmouth only eight years of his life, when he was a young man fishing with the menhaden fleet. Now he has heart trouble and can do little.

Cannon grins as Gaskill kids Piggot about his cooking and the time he was away and got stabbed and, even worse, almost married. Gaskill relishes telling how Piggot, when his bride-to-be got him to the church, decided to head for the nearest exit and left "winder and all."

"I'm telling all on him," Gaskill says, grinning.

Piggot changes the subject, begins talking about Portsmouth. He's never thought of leaving, he says. "This is my home, you see." He could never live in a city, he says. "All that pushing and shoving . . ." He shakes his head. None of that in Portsmouth.

He longingly recalls when Portsmouth was still a town. "Son, this used to be a great land, a great place over here . . ." His voice trails away.

Time comes for Lum Gaskill to return to Ocracoke.

"I'll get you that chicken feed if I can get it," he tells Fred Cannon, as Cannon strikes out for the hike back home.

Piggot asks about fish, and Gaskill says he got some blues recently and his wife has just salted some puppy drum.

"Which would you rather have," Piggot calls to Miss Dixon, "a blue fish or a piece of drum?" He speaks loudly, almost yelling.

"Don't matter," she says, her sole offering to this day's conservation.

"Bring me a couple of bluefish," Piggot says.

In the skiff, heading back to Ocracoke, Lum Gaskill recalls tales of the old sea captains who lived in Portsmouth in the days of the four-masted ships.

"That was a sea-going place, that Portsmouth," he says. "I'm going to find out all about it and write me a book on it, I am. That's the reason I got this job."

November, 1968
Portsmouth Island, North Carolina

Just Folks

Lillian Babb, a Portsmouth resident to the end, died in January 1969. The following year, Fred Cannon's small fishing boat was found adrift in the sound near Ocracoke. He was presumed drowned. His body was never found. That same year, Henry Piggot fell ill and moved across the sound to Ocracoke to be nearer a doctor. He died in a hospital in Elizabeth City in January, 1971. The National Park Service, which now controls Portsmouth Island, has since named one of its work boats in his memory. Marion Babb and Eleanor Dixon moved from Portsmouth shortly after Henry's death. They live now in Beaufort.

Henry Shirtz
Middle-Aged Beginner

The *Wolftrap* went out on Tuesday. Normally, she would have been gone a week or more and come back riding low in the water, her belly filled with thousands of pounds of fish.

But on the second day out a net snagged bottom and severely bent a boom. She was leaking, too, and needed to be put in the boatyard to be recaulked. So on Thursday night the *Wolftrap* chugged back up the sound to her dock at Wanchese, holding her bent boom like a broken arm.

It had been a lousy trip, the crew agreed. There were only 4,000 pounds of blackbacks, cousins of the flounder, in the hold. And to the crew every fish is money in the pocket. Few fish, few dollars.

If things had been going right, a shore crew would have been waiting to unload the catch, but things weren't going right, of course. So on Friday morning, the crew came to get the small catch out of the boat, into boxes, and onto a truck bound for a processing plant in Elizabeth City, 70 miles away.

That is, two-thirds of the crew came. The other member had said to hell with it and was home drunk. Henry Shirtz laughed about that. He knows all about boozing.

The *Wolftrap*'s deck was a tangle of nets, ropes, ball weights, winches and other paraphernalia. The captain's two young sons ranged over the deck playing with small lobsters and crabs that had been dredged up in the nets.

The captain, Monty O'Neal, a lean, angular man with a Marine recruit haircut, the bottom half of his weather-proof fishing suit pulled up over a red sport shirt, was standing in a trough on the dock shoveling fish into a hanging scale, then dumping them into wooden crates.

A couple of other fishermen had come over to help. ("They'd do the same for us.") Henry Shirtz was in the hold of the weathered, aging boat. He shoveled the fish into a large wire basket using a big coal shovel. One of the helping fishermen guided the basket to the dock where it was dunked into a huge wooden barrel filled with soupy water. The captain dumped the basket into the trough and then it came back for Henry Shirtz to fill again.

Henry Shirtz was sweating. A day's growth of white beard

15

bristled on his bronzed face. He looked up into the light streaming into the hold and winced.

"I'm in the embryo stage of fishing right now," he said.

He is 52, and a few years earlier, if somebody had told him he'd someday be shoveling blackbacks into a wire basket in the hold of a leaky old fishing boat in a village called Wanchese on Roanoke Island, North Carolina — he'd never even heard of Wanchese — he'd have told them they were crazy. But here he was, shoveling, sweating, and no doubt about it, a fisherman.

Not so long before, Henry Shirtz had been a mechanical engineer for a big company in New Jersey. He made much money and spent a lot of time on his sailboat.

"Then my wife died five years ago," he said. "I became a drunk."

He lost his job, took what money he had left and joined a partner in a fishing boat. On his first fishing trip, the boat hit a sandbar and sank off Ocracoke island. Henry Shirtz and his partner were able to fashion a raft and escape. They drifted in the cold January night and were just about to give up when they saw a light flash not far away.

The light was in the cabin of Fred Cannon on Portsmouth Island.

"Fred saved our lives," Henry Shirtz was saying. "We ran in the water to the cabin, hadn't had nothing to eat. He fed us some beans. Boy, it tasted like steak."

Henry Shirtz had now lost everything, and like many other men who have been shipwrecked on the Outer Banks, he decided to stay. "I liked it there," he explained, "just stayed." He kicked the booze, married a Hatteras woman (his captain's mother) and signed on the *Wolftrap*.

"I decided I'd like to learn something about this business. Good buck to be made in it."

It was almost noon. Henry Shirtz's wife had come down to the dock. "I'm just waiting for my husband to get out of that hold and come home for some lunch," she said, as she watched the last basketful of blackbacks swing off the boat.

Henry Shirtz emerged from the hold a few minutes later. "Hi, hon," he called. He wiped the sweat from his brow, got out of his wet gear, climbed off the *Wolftrap*, and arm-in-arm, he and his wife walked off the dock, past the group of little stores and fish houses, and disappeared around the curve toward home.

June, 1969
Wanchese, North Carolina

Clarke Willcox
Living with a Ghost

You cannot see the old house from the road. The driveway cuts through the thick wall of undergrowth and circles around to the house, which is hidden amongst the giant cedars and huge live oaks, squat and gnarled with thick spreading arms. The house has big white pillars, each cut from a single tree, and it faces the marsh grasses and shallow waters of the narrow sound. From the front porch, you can look across the sound and see the little spit of sand where vacation cottages and condominiums keep going up on the ocean. Sometimes the old man looks across there and sadly shakes his head.

He had come up from the greenhouse and was waiting for us. His name is Clarke Willcox and he is 78 years old. He is slightly stooped, and despite a touch of arthritis ("I developed arthritis two or three months ago, right at the time they started streaking," he tells us with a little grin. "I tell folks that the Lord gave me this arthritis in my right knee to keep me from streaking."), he has remained spirited and active.

"I have a nursery and I have a garden," he said, "and I have a wife and she finds plenty for me to do."

My friends and I had come to hear a ghost story, but first we sat in rocking chairs on the porch and talked. We talked about the house, about history, the area, his life, and about many other things, for Clarke Willcox has a keen mind, a quick wit and a wide knowledge of many subjects.

He first came to Murrell's Inlet in 1903. He was seven and he came with his family in wagons. It took them two days to make the 56 miles from Marion, where his father was a shoe merchant. They stayed two weeks.

"We'd never seen the ocean," he recalled. "We got a love for the place in that two weeks."

At that time, the northeast corner of South Carolina was still mostly wilderness, cut off from the rest of the state by water. Myrtle Beach was just another isolated strip of sand. Only the big plantation from the previous century kept the area from being total wilderness. Clarke Willcox's father bought a small piece of land on the sound for $25 and spent another $500 building a small

17

house on it. For the next seven years he brought his family to it each summer.

In 1910, the house where we now sat on the porch came up for sale. It was the main house of an old plantation called the Hermitage, that had been built in 1849 by the Flagg family, a family of doctors descended from the first surgeon general of the Continental Army. Clarke Willcox's father bought the house and 937 acres of land for $10,000.

As a young man, Clarke had come to the plantation one summer and "made a crop," fighting the mosquitoes and bugs and free-ranging livestock to grow cotton, corn and tobacco. It had been very strenuous work, not quite what he had in mind for a livelihood. He returned to Marion, opened a grocery store, and remained for 38 years, marrying and rearing four daughters in that time. Meanwhile, his father had been living on the plantation and selling the land a piece at a time. When Clarke Willcox inherited it in 1944, there was not much left. Another 10 years passed before he decided to move to the old house.

"We've been here for 18 years now," he was saying. "I told folks I was coming down here to die, and if I'd known it was going to be so much fun, we'd have come earlier."

He planted a garden, started a nursery and began doing a little writing. He would write little poems and stick them in his pocket. His wife would find them and put them into a drawer. One day he realized he had enough to publish a book. He called the collection *The Musings of a Hermit*. He had 1,500 copies printed, and after he had sold those, he had 3,000 more printed, then 5,000 more, and another 5,000. Those are almost gone now. "These poems I've been writing, some of 'em are pretty good and some of 'em are pretty corny," he said. "Some people wonder why I put some of 'em in there. I put 'em in there because I wrote 'em."

With the success of his poems, he moved on to other forms and put out a book of reminiscences and history. He did not have to look far for material, because for the past 18 years he has been living in the same house with one of the best known ghosts in the country.

Clarke Willcox never knows who may show up at his door. Unannounced visitors come all the time, especially in the vacation months. One day he went to the door and found the movie actress Patricia Neal standing there with her writer husband. All the visitors come for the same reason. They want to know about Alice Flagg.

Clarke Willcox and his wife, Lillian, accept them graciously. They take them on tours of the house, and Clarke tells them the story of Alice, just as he told us as we sat on the porch.

Alice was the daughter of a doctor, the granddaughter of a doctor, and her brothers were doctors, too. Her father was dead when she was sent away to a girls' school in Charleston. She liked it there. She did well and was popular with the other girls, who made her the belle of the spring ball. She was very happy. But not all of her happiness was due to her situation at school. She had fallen in love with a young man in the turpentine business and they had become secretly engaged. She wore the ring he had given her on a chain around her neck, being careful to keep it concealed under her clothing.

"She knew if her brother knew she was engaged without his permission, he would raise the devil," Clarke Willcox said. She knew, too, that her brother, now the family head, would consider somebody in the turpentine business beneath her station.

Then Alice was taken ill and became delirious with fever. A courier was sent by horse to fetch her brother, who set out for Charleston by carriage. The trip took four days and required the crossing of five rivers. He brought Alice home to the big plantation house that had just been built. She was in a coma when they arrived.

Her brother found the ring as he was examining her. He became angry about it, took it outside and threw it into the sound. When Alice regained consciousness, she missed the ring and asked about it. Her brother denied any knowledge of it. She feared she had lost it and begged her cousins to search for it. She never recovered it, of course, and soon died, broken-hearted over its loss. She was 16 and the year was 1849. She was buried in the yard until her mother could be brought from the mountains, where she had fled to avoid the malaria season. Then Alice's body was moved to the cemetery of a small Episcopal church near Pawley's Island, several miles away.

It did not take long for the story of Alice Flagg to spread, and it did not take long either for people to begin to see her ghost. Her grave, set under moss-draped oaks in the old graveyard, is covered by a heavy slab of stone bearing the single word, "Alice." It is a regular tourist attraction. A path is worn around it, and many persons claim to have found gardenias, Alice's favorite flower, adorning the grave in the middle of winter.

Clarke Willcox heard the story of Alice when he first came to Murrell's Inlet. "When I was a kid it was going around, but it's going stronger today than it did then," he said.

An aunt once came to visit his father and stayed in the room where Alice had died. She was sitting at a dresser mirror one morning getting ready to go down to breakfast when she saw the image of a young girl in a white dress appear in the mirror. She thought it was one of the children who had been sent to call her to breakfast, but when she turned around no one was there. That caused quite a commotion in the house.

"To her dying day, she said she was never more amazed in her life," Clarke Willcox said.

The year before, he was sitting on his porch one day when a man drove up. They got to talking and the man told him he had come earlier without finding anybody at home. But as he started to drive away, he saw a lovely young girl dressed in white standing in the garden. He stopped to talk to her but she disappeared. When he got out of the car, he couldn't find her, he said.

Encounters with Alice happen more often at her grave. "They have some amazing experiences there," Clarke Willcox said. "They see and feel and they hear . . . They see this form coming toward them and they hear these sounds and all that kind of thing. We have them come up here sometime in that frame of mind and they are very upset."

Visitors always ask him if he believes in the ghost. "I tell them of course I do," he said, chuckling. "I tell them I wouldn't live in a house with just one woman. One of them's a spirit and I don't have to send her to the beauty parlor or zip her up."

But he admits with a shake of the head that despite all his years in the house, he has never seen Alice. "It's a feeling with us. Sometimes I go up to her room to close the windows and there is definitely a presence there. The feeling is more intense really than the fact that you saw something."

May, 1974
Murrell's Inlet, South Carolina

Lee Dough
The Man Who Lassoed a Whale

We sat in a glider on the screened porch, the old man and I.

"The next time, if I reach the next time, I'll be 74," he said. He didn't seem to care if he reached it or not.

His hair was white, his nose bulbous and red. The skin on his neck was leathery and wrinkled. His hands were big and rough, his arms scaly. He raised them slowly. "Warts and mold eat an old man up," he said.

The eyes. They said everything about Lee Dough, all at once. Weak, watery, red, despairing and lonely, yet inexplicably strong and piercing. He focused them directly on mine and sat silently. I fidgeted, looked away.

"You can't find a man that can look you straight in the eye," he said.

"It's hard," I said, nodding agreement.

"You married?" he asked.

I said I was, that I had a little boy, three years old. I grinned.

"You take care of them," he demanded, the eyes still on mine. Suddenly, he turned away. "I lost my partner," he said softly. "The 17th of last February was a year, next February will be two."

We sat without speaking for a few minutes.

"You see that old rosebush at the corner of the house? That's some history for you. My old granddaddy brought the setting of that rosebush from the West Indies islands. My old granddaddy sailed a two-masted ship. You know where the Lost Colony is? That was his place. That's where I spent a happy boyhood. The first land sold for that Lost Colony was my old granddaddy's."

It was the whale I was interested in mostly, I finally told him. What about it? Was it true?

He fixed his eyes hard on me again. It seemed minutes before he spoke.

"If ever in my life," he began slowly, "I ever told a fish lie, I don't know when it was. I hate a damn liar."

Proof, he said, he would produce. When he was ready. "I'm not one for advertising," he said.

We went into the living room. "Forty-three years I been living here," he was saying. "Now I'm all alone in this big old house.

21

Not even a mouse in here. If they was I'd chase him down."

The picture of the boat was on the wall, a small white fishing boat, the *Libby-D*, bobbing in the sound. "She was built in '36," he said proudly. "Me and my daddy and two brothers built it. If you can find a piece of rotten wood in it, I'll eat it.

"You know who that is?" he asked, pointing to a picture of a young man. "Twenty-two years old," he said. "I was all wool and a yard wide."

For years Captain Lee Dough took out fishing parties. "I used to drive a T-Model truck over here to Point Harbor. I had parties I would take out for eight days at a time. Now they fight over parties for half a day."

Three years earlier, Lee Dough was hit by a car near his house. "I'm all crippled up," he said. "I can't fish no more." The *Libby-D* is tied up. He can't find a captain for her.

We sat for a long time looking through a drawerful of old photographs, pictures of fishing parties and happy times.

"I've done hit the low mark," he was saying. "My time is behind me. What have I got to live for but memories?"

He put the pictures away and led me to a bedroom. There on the wall, eyes bulging, was the whale.

He took the picture down carefully, looked it over, and passed it to me.

"I don't want no advertising," he said. "I don't need no advertising. But you can say this, that I, Lee Dough, am the only guide on the Atlantic Coast who ever took out a sport fishing party and came back with a whale."

It had been about 25 years earlier. The ton-heavy mammal was wallowing in Oregon Inlet. "Tied a damn rope around his tail," he said, grinning. "You know where the skeleton of that fish is? In the Mariners Museum in Boston."

Outside, we stood on the steps. I was ready to leave. Lee Dough fixed me in his gaze. "You take care of that little wife," he said. "Be good to her. And that little boy."

I nodded. We looked out over the yard.

"My partner's gone," he said. "She liked this yard. I kept it up for her, but I ain't able now."

September, 1968
Manteo, North Carolina

Wimpy Lassiter
Pool Shooter

The house at 500 Pearl Street is like many others in Elizabeth City — old, two-story frame dwellings with big, vine-draped front porches. It is a couple of blocks from the downtown business district, and like a lot of other houses, it needs a paint job. Somebody started painting it once, yellow. They painted around the front porch and quit and now even that paint is pale and peeling. This for years has been the Lassiter home. Luther Lassiter was born here. He still lives here, single, age 49.

Luther Lassiter shoots pool. That's it. "I just played pool all my life," he says. "I live off of my fat brother that just met you at the door." He smiles faintly. It should be mentioned he also drives a new white Cadillac.

This day he is not feeling well. "Feel like hell. Sick at my stomach."

Somehow he does not fit in this house with its almost dainty decor. He is short, pudgy. His hair is white, his eyes droopy, his pants baggy.

He slouches in a chair. "Pool hasn't gotten the right start yet," he says. "A pool player's got a hard way to go to make a living."

Luther Lassiter is considered to be one of the three best professional straight pool players in the world. He has won so many world and national championship titles that he can't remember the exact number. Now he is waiting for a call and he has barely started talking when the phone rings.

It is Joe Balsis, another of the three, calling from Pennsylvania. Lassiter has a long and animated conservation:

". . . What the hell's going on? Out in Vegas? Damn, that'd be fine . . .

"We've got to explain. The better players have got to have some expenses in coming tournaments . . .

"Oh, no, he's going to lose it to me before this year's out. Well, he's that way, you know. He's a funny guy. You know, you're like me. You'll play. You don't care whether you get beat or not. You're just trying to make a few bucks . . .

"He's made more out of pool than anybody I've ever seen in my life. It's ridiculous . . . Old friend, he writes me. I've got a banana split from him in my whole life. One banana split . . .

"Well, Joe, what do you think? Go ahead and play in January? Maybe next year they'll see the damn light. That's good enough. Hell. We'd be a sucker to let this go by . . ."

He hangs up and flops back into the chair. "Promoters make the money," he says.

Luther Lassiter began shooting pool when he was 13. "Right up the street here," he says. "In a boy's back yard. He's a doctor now. He had built a four-pocket table."

From there he moved up to the YMCA. "Been playing everybody who could play since I was 17 years old," he recalls. By that age he had become a "player beater."

"People used to come after me," he explains.

He also admits to some hustling in his younger years, "But I never tried to play anybody who couldn't play." He lapses into reminiscence about those years. "I won a bunch of money up in Mooresville. That was in the war years. Bigshot bootlegger. He ran all the liquor down to Charlotte. I didn't know who I was playing or I'd really made me some money."

He spent four and a half years in the Coast Guard and went back to pool when he got out. Did he ever consider any other career? "Only thing that ever crossed my mind was maybe a surgeon." His family offered to send him to college but he declined. "Pool had me!" he says. "Hell, I wanted to play pool."

He became a professional in 1953, the same year a big sporting goods firm dropped its sponsorship of the professional pool circuit. There are still only a few pool tournaments a year and the prize money isn't big. "If you come in second, you about break even," he says.

Once he practiced four hours a day, six days a week. Once he shot for two and a half hours without missing a shot; finally, tiring and thinking he might never miss, he quit.

He doesn't practice much any more, he says, although he did get a pool table a few years back and built a little house out back for it, where he sometimes shoots with his nephews. The truth is, he says, he's sick of pool.

"Hell, I'm 49. It takes a lot of energy to shoot pool. I don't have any enthusiasm for the game. That left me 10, 15 years ago."

He isn't sick enough of it to quit, though. Not yet. "It's about all I know how to do. Hell, I'm not married. It makes a big difference . . . it doesn't matter if you make a living. You can bum around. I'm not sure it's not the best life."

November, 1968
Elizabeth City, North Carolina

25

Mary Sams
Lady of Leisure

As a young woman, she cavorted in Paris in the '20s, keeping a string of beaus, pretending to be a sculptress, having tea with Alice B. Toklas, dinner with Scott and Zelda.

As a society matron in Atlanta, she had nurses for her children ("I do not believe in togetherness; it's absolutely uncivilized.") and a battery of servants.

"I simply can't understand how any woman can survive raising children without the buffer of domestic help," she says. "It's the only thing young people should borrow money for. They don't need an automobile or a stereo or all that slop. They need servants to make them live a fairly civilized life. I never had less than three servants. We were ladies of leisure."

Mary Sams is 71 now, and she lives, servantless, in a light and airy apartment on the second floor of an old house on Port Republic Street in Beaufort, South Carolina, with a calico cat named Lillian Hellman and a monstrous split-leaf philodendron she calls the Orphan Child.

The cat, a stray, was rescued from a snow bank in Connecticut. Mary Sams keeps up a running conversation with her: "Yes, Miss Hellman, we absolutely agree with you. You're a beautiful cat . . . She's very fond of men, Lillian Hellman is. There are a great many people who want to be reincarnated as that cat."

The philodendron she acquired when she moved to Beaufort in the spring of 1971, following the death of her husband, Robert, a prominent lawyer. She was looking at apartments, and at one she found a young woman packing sorrowfully. The young woman's Marine husband had been sent to Vietnam, and she was moving back home with her parents. There wasn't room for her prized philodendron. Would Mary consider giving it a good home?

"It was like somebody handing over their child," she says. "What could you do?"

The plant spent summers on her broad porch until it grew too big to get through the door. "Now it sulks all summer and pokes the windows out trying to get out," she says.

It has taken over a good portion of her parlor. When she seated a guest near it recently, he glanced nervously over his shoulder at it and asked, "Chained, I presume?"

26

Mary Sams chose to live in Beaufort for several reasons. She wanted to live in a small town; her husband's family had come from Beaufort and she had family connections here. Beaufort also had a lot of history into which she could look.

"I'm absolutely nuts on the subject of history," she says. "It's my golf game. I've been a history buff for as long as I can remember."

Another reason she chose Beaufort was that is convenient to Savannah and Charleston, cities rife with charm and history. "If the fuzz are resting quietly, I can get to Charleston in an hour and 10 minutes," she says.

There are some, Mary knows, who would be just as happy if she had chosen some other place to settle. "I'm afraid I exhaust people. Most people here want their history fancied up. Occasionally, there is a difference of opinion on these subjects."

Differences of opinion have cropped up on more than history. Mary Sams has made something of a gadfly of herself in and around Beaufort, and her stinger is sharp. She has been critical of everything from Beaufort's new waterfront (" . . . Hideous. When I saw the plans for this waterfront in the city hall, I fell down on the floor in a fit.") to the quality of the area's men ("This is a lousy town for man hunting. The men who show up around here are lazy.").

Few people know Beaufort and environs better than Mary Sams. "I'm an island roamer," she says. "I haunt things." Once while roaming on a nearby island, keeping a careful watch for snakes, she wandered into a large patch of marijuana. "If you could have seen me coming out of there, you'd have thought there were cobras in there," she says, laughing. "Dozens and dozens of cobras. No place for Mama to be, playing in the marijuana."

A tour of Beaufort with Mary Sams includes much more than the local museum and old houses of which Beaufort is so proud ("I know a great deal more about these houses than most of the people who live here."). She is certain to point out the giant live oaks along the waterfront the city has killed by paving parking spaces too close.

"I am really distressed by the loss of these trees," she says as she wheels her car past a public flower bed that catches her eye. "Oh, if that isn't the most godawful thing. What garden club has spawned that visual pollution?"

"That's the whore houses," she says, passing one seedy area, "and that's very integrated."

27

Just Folks

She is also apt to point out where the homosexual Marines from nearby Parris Island hang out and the homes of several voodoo witch doctors who practice in the area, most of whom she knows. She has, in fact, been a client of Dr. Buzzard on more than one occasion. She once bought a root from him to place a hex on a local official for whom she had a particular dislike. That very day, she says, the official fell under investigation and was ousted not long afterward.

She stops her car in mid-street to decry the metal-frame, double-pane windows installed in one historic house, and a small car behind toots.

"Oh, shut up!" she calls to the driver. "Why do you buy a baby car like that if you're not going to go by somebody?"

On the back seat, Lillian Hellman stretches. "Are you getting tired, Miss Hellman? Well, we'll just take you home." Back in her apartment, Mary Sams takes one look at the Orphan Child hunkering in one end of her parlor and recoils.

"Oh, she's adding a new leaf, dammit!"

November, 1978
Beaufort, South Carolina

Texes Sears
Open for Business

One side of the building has collapsed, the roof gone, walls caved in. At first glance, it would seem the old store is only a decaying relic, long abandoned.

But then in that front window . . . a flicker of light, a flash of greenery.

Push the heavy wood door, adorned with faded advertisements, and it opens. Step inside and step back in time. On the dusty shelves of Sears Store some merchandise has rested since the '20s, probably longer.

Texes Sears, short, plump, white-haired, emerges smiling from the shadows behind the counter, wiping her hands on her apron, apologizing for her appearance.

"I've been cooking," she says.

She has not been expecting strangers. They rarely call at Sears Store anymore.

Once, long ago, Sears Store was the center of commerce for Sladesville, a farming and fishing village on a branch of the Pungo River in coastal Hyde County. Texes Sears doesn't know how long the store has been in business.

"Good gosh, now you ask me something I can't tell you . . . They's some says it's a hundred, some says it's over a hundred year old."

Her father, Napoleon Bonaparte Sears, a peddler, bought it about 1912. She took over after his death in 1936 and has operated it since.

"You wonder why I never got married, don't you?" she asks, then smiles. "You know there's a sayin': if you get married you can't love but one. If you stay single you can love 'em all. Oh, I had plenty of chances."

The store has fallen around her, year by year, board by board. Her Uncle John once lived in the rooms on the other side of the building, but after his death in 1955 she wasn't able to keep that part in repair any longer and it gradually collapsed.

"The worst of it went in that hard wind we had in the spring," she says.

The upstairs living and storage quarters were abandoned, too, as Texes Sears retreated, shoring up with cedar posts. For the past

29

five years she has lived in the dark and sagging section that was for so long the community store, there amidst the jumble of ancient merchandise, just she, her cat, her windowful of green plants and her calendar pictures of Jesus. And somehow, through it all, she has managed to stay open for business.

But there is precious little of that. Most of the village commerce has been usurped by a newer store with modern gas pumps on the corner across the road. Texes Sears mainly sells soft drinks, candy, packaged cookies and crackers now.

"Why do I stay open? Because I want something to do. Don't want to give up till I have to. I get along. I get along. This keeps me super . . . You don't know super? Keeps you young, keeps you from gettin' old."

There are other reasons, too. That newer store across the road may have taken away the business, but Sears Store still serves as the community visiting place, the place where people come to sit on upturned milk crates around the woodburner to talk about the weather, the fishing, the new preacher, the courting habits of the young people, to tease and joke with Texes Sears.

"Well, I'll give you an idee, Cap'n, how old she is," says Cap'n Will O'Neal, smiling at Texes Sears. "She was on the basketball team in 19 and 14."

"In that little teddy bear suit," says her friend, Clafton Williams, grinning.

Which prompts a discussion of changes in fashion among those assembled around the woodburner on this rainy afternoon. But the conservation soon turns to reminiscences of Sears Store.

"Used to be a molasses barrel set right there," says Clafton Williams. "Get them ol' molasses out of there, boy . . ."

"Vinegar barrel," says somebody.

"Apple butter by the bucket . . ." offers another.

"Kerosene barrel set out by the door," adds Texes Sears.

"I used to ride a horse out here and get a nickel's worth of ice to take home to make ice tea," says Wilbur Fisher.

"Yeah, and it'd be about melted by the time you got it home, wouldn't it," says Texes Sears.

"No, not the way I rode that ol' mule," he replies, laughing.

No day passes that a group does not form around the woodburner, and from them Texes Sears takes sustenance. A few years back, when she fell and broke her hip, it was suggested she ought to recuperate in a nursing home. But she insisted on going back to the store.

"Told 'em I'd fare just as good here," she says. "Had good

friends, good neighbors."

"Yeah," says Clafton Williams, grinning mischievously, "I have to stay here and look after 'er."

"Tuh!" she says. "He can't even look after himself."

"But we have a good time," he says.

"Oh, we do," she agrees. "Ain't no need in dyin' till you have to, is there?"

November, 1977
Sladesville, North Carolina

Case Van Staalduinen
Flower Farmer

The fields stretch for miles, rich and black and flat, broken only by distant tree lines, neat farmhouses, and the sharp instrusion of tall silos. It is easy to see why this place came to be called Terra Ciea, heavenly earth.

In past springs and early summers, these fields were alive with color. That has changed. But the names on the mailboxes haven't. Van Gyzen. Van Wyk. Van Staalduinen. Unmistakably Dutch.

In the '30s and early '40s, a group of Dutch immigrants settled here in coastal Beaufort County. Lured by the rich soil, they came to grow the flowers of the old country: tulips, gladiolas, irises, daffodils, hyacinths, peonies, crocuses. At the peak of their production, in the late '40s and early '50s, there were 30 growers with more than 500 acres of flowers.

The Dutch community remains, held together by a church and private school. But corn and soybeans abound in fields where flowers once blossomed. A couple of families still grow a few acres of daffodils and peonies, but only Case Van Staalduinen still grows flowers on a large scale.

"It's like produce," he says. "It's very risky. You don't know whether you're going to make it or not. And it's dirty, hard work."

But it was more than risk and hard work that drove the other growers out. Labor became expensive and hard to get. Their children grew up here, then were lured away by easier, more lucrative occupations. Small growers found they could not compete with larger growers. One by one they dropped away, and Case Van Staalduinen often bought them out.

He sits at his dining room table, thumbing through a family photo album, while his wife, Holly, bakes a traditional Dutch pastry for their son's birthday. Case's mother prepared the album and gave it to him, a family history in pictures. Central to that history are flowers.

"We've been in it for a while," he says. "There's my great-grandfather. He's in his tulip patch in the old country."

The pictures flip past: his father and uncles in their greenhouse before his father decided to emigrate from Holland to Canada . . . his mother, himself, eight brothers and sisters on the deck of the

32

Veendam sailing for Canada in 1939 . . . three of his brothers in 1943, their first year on the farm at Terra Ciea . . . the first crop of tulip bulbs at Terra Ciea, 1944 . . . his mother and father in a field of daffodils at Easter before his father's death two years ago at age 79. All the pictures have been neatly captioned by his mother.

"Flowers," says Case, "that was all my dad knew."

His father, Leonard, had followed his own father and grandfather into the flower business in Holland. He shipped bulbs to England and Germany. But as World War II approached, he saw no future in Holland and took his family to Canada.

"Broke, just as well be honest about it," says Case. "They were broke. My dad would shovel coal for $2 a day and run a flower farm at night. That's tough."

"Us kids, we used to peddle flowers. You know, go to houses. I remember going to houses and peddlin' 'em a quarter a bunch."

But the growing season was short in Canada. A friend of Leonard Staalduinen's had begun growing flowers at Terra Ciea in the mid-'30s, and Leonard Staalduinen came to join him as soon as immigration opened up.

Gradually, he expanded, renting land, buying more land with profits, buying out other growers. Case joined him and took over when his father died. He now has 200 acres of flowers. He spends much of his time on the road — buying, selling, working deals — while his brother, Bill, oversees the farm. Of 10 children, only they remain in the flower business.

Despite the long tradition, Case Van Staalduinen is quick to say he has no sentimental attachments to flower growing, that he could leave it without regrets if something more lucrative came along.

"I could do it. I think so. If I had to pick tulips . . . I've picked enough tulips in my day. I wouldn't care if I never picked another tulip. I like tulips, don't get me wrong. I just don't want to get out there in the field and eat dirt no more.

"Sometimes you wish you could get away from all of it, but I can't quit the flower business because I got so much money invested in it. I can't get out.

"Volume is the only way you can make it. You can't make it from small acreage anymore. The small guy gets out because he can't afford it and we gotta go on because we've got so much money invested."

He spends a lot of time traveling around the country buying out stock from small growers getting out. "I like to turn volume. I can travel, go to this grower and that grower. I don't guess I could ever quit the bulb business. I would stay in sales or something."

Case Van Staalduinen in 48. He has five children, the eldest a son, 12. Would he encourage any of them to follow him into the flower business?

"I don't know," he says. "I don't think I'd be able to talk my kids into going into the bulb business. But now my wife, she could."

April, 1978
Terra Ciea, North Carolina

Les and Sally Moore
Pioneers

They came like pioneers, motivated by the same dreams that pioneers have always dreamed: to get away, to build new opportunities.

And now they must face the harsh truth that pioneers inevitably face. Time and events have caught up with them.

Sally Moore smiles and her whole face smiles, a maze of crinkles. "We have completed 15 years," she says. "We're starting our 16th."

For all those years, Les and Sally Moore have been the only permanent residents of Cape Lookout (the Coast Guard station has a small detachment of men who are rotated regularly). They have had 20 miles of primitive island to range over, all the solitude they ever dreamed about, but surprisingly, they find they have to explain to a lot of people why they chose such a life. Sally tries.

"Well, I guess we're just outback people to begin with. It was getting too crowded on Atlantic Beach."

Les and Sally met in Morehead City during World War II. She had lived in the area all her life. He had been born and reared in Idaho. He now likes to tell people that "I was just born a long ways from home." He was in the service when they met and married, and after the war, they opened a small motel on Atlantic Beach.

Cape Lookout seemed the natural place to go when they began to feel crowded on Atlantic Beach. It was close by but it was wild and isolated and it offered the potential to support a small business because of the regular traffic of sport fishermen in the area.

Les and Sally sold their motel and bought nearly six acres at the cape, not far from the lighthouse. It was high land for the Outer Banks, a good eight feet above extreme high water.

They had built a small houseboat and they lived on that as they began to build their new home. They did all the work themselves, hauling materials from Morehead City on a barge. They started from the water and worked inward, building a dock before starting their first building. It was hard work.

During the process, a hurricane named Donna caught them on the island and gave them a good idea of what their new life might

hold in store. They rode it out in an old fishing shack that stood on their property.

"It was cotton-pickin' bad," Sally recalls. "It was a bad night. I think it was the hardest wind I've seen in my life."

Their complex now includes the dock, the main building that serves as store and home, four adjoining cabins that they rent on a daily basis, usually to fishermen, several out buildings and a field full of fishermen's jalopies.

Business has been good enough to allow them to stay, and Les and Sally seldom leave the island for the simple reason they can't think of any place they'd rather be, even for a short time. Les hasn't even been to Morehead City in more than two years, except once when he had to pass through on the way to an appointment at a veterans' hospital. They keep in touch with the rest of the world by radio.

Les and Sally have weathered with the elements, their skin becoming leathery and deeply lined, and as they weathered it was almost as if they became part of the island itself. They love it deeply.

"This is the only place outside the Florida Keys that you can see the sun come up out of the ocean and go down over the ocean," Sally is saying. "This is the most southeastern point in the United States."

She is tending the store on this day. Les is out helping another man build a house on the island. The store offers soft drinks, beer, sandwiches, some canned foods, fishing tackle, and assorted odds and ends. Mostly, though, it offers shelter for the great (and not for sale) collection of beautiful old bottles, shells, anchors, driftwood and other treasures Les and Sally have gathered from the beaches through the years.

As Les and Sally became a part of their island, they became acutely aware of their place in it and their responsibility to it.

"Ever since this country has been here," Sally says, "people have taken from it and never put anything back. Well, we're trying to put something back. We planted sea oats seed, American beach grass, up here where people said it wouldn't grow, and yucca. We planted trees galore. All the tall pines you see, we planted.

"They're all doing well, and we've got the prettiest crop of cedars you ever saw coming up from the *birds*. That's why we get so cotton pickin' mad when we see people over here with guns."

People with guns come all the time. They come to shoot birds and other creatures, to kill just for fun. "They kill all kinds of birds," Sally says. She and Les have no special authority on the island but they do feel free to administer harsh lectures to the gun toters, which they do whenever they spot them. Their concern for the island's wildlife extends beyond the birds, however. Consider the turtles.

Every year when the loggerhead turtles, lumbering giants weighing up to 900 pounds, wallow ashore to lay their eggs, Les and Sally get up early each morning and scour the beaches for signs that they have arrived. The turtles sometimes lay their eggs in places where the tide will wash over the nests, and if that happens the eggs won't hatch. If the tide doesn't get the eggs, gulls or people often do. "Hardly any of them ever hatch and get to the water," says Sally.

Les and Sally see to it that the turtles at least get a chance to live. They find the nests, dig up the eggs and rebury them in a safe spot next to their store. Then, just before they're supposed to hatch, they dig them up again, bring them inside and let them hatch in an ice chest. Late at night, Les takes the little turtles out to sea and sets them on their way with a big headstart in life.

They have been doing that for years, and Sally keeps careful records. "We've just had 135 that hatched out," she says thumbing through her record book. "Let's see how many eggs we've got left . . . 556 eggs left. We hope to get at least 500 live turtles out of that and we might just do it. They're just as cute as they can be. They're precious . . . and they're becoming extinct. People are taking the beaches from them. All of our wildlife is like that. Nature is just being taken away from them. They're just as much a part of this world as we are, and they've got a right to live."

Soon, though, the turtles probably will have to fend for themselves once again. Les and Sally doubt they'll be able to stay at Cape Lookout. The island is to become a national seashore and their property is to be taken. They don't like it very much.

"I'd love for it to stay the way it is," Sally says. "There are few places left that aren't ruled and regulated to death, and I suppose this is the last outpost where there's good fishing."

But they know it is coming and that there is nothing they can do about it. Now, they say, they're just in a state of limbo, not knowing exactly what will happen or when. They may be given lifetime rights to remain on their property after it is taken, but they won't be able to operate their business. And without the income from the store and cottages, they say, they won't be able to stay. Beyond that, they have no idea where they would go or what they would do.

"I don't know," Sally says, shaking her head. "Where *would* we go? I don't know. We'd be like fish out of water. There isn't any place."

August, 1975
Cape Lookout, North Carolina

In the spring of 1979, nearly a year after Les and Sally Moore were forced out of their home at Cape Lookout, I visited them at the house they had bought in Morehead City and found them still living out of boxes.

"We're sorta lost, Jerry," Les said.

We sat at the kitchen table, surrounded by stacks of bulging cardboard boxes, and talked about adjusting.

"The sky," Sally said. "I miss the sky. We used to have the whole sky."

"Here we have to look straight up," Les said. "Don't get us wrong. It's pretty here. We got some little squirrels about to eat us out of house and home."

The house they bought is well away from the water. It is small and old and not much to look at, but the lot has huge live oak trees and room enough for a garden, something Sally couldn't have on the island. Les has been ripping the house apart to remodel it, adding a new room at the back for Sally's shell and bottle collections and other beachcombing treasures.

"I went back to the cape about a month after we left," Sally told me, "and of course I cried and it tore me all to pieces."

Neither has been back since. They have, in fact, been avoiding the water. "Haven't even been fishing," said Sally. "The water is going to have to become separate. If we can't divorce ourselves from that water, then we just can't get along."

"Coming inland like this makes the whole basis of life completely different," Les said. "We had lived on the water since '46."

Sally looked at Les and tried to smile. "When we first left, I was awfully concerned that Les would have difficulty getting adjusted and, by golly, here it is me. I've taken a sewing course and started a garden. Try to get an interest every day.

"But every full moon I can feel it. I'll be sittin' here and say, 'It must be full moon,' and I'll look at the calendar and it is and I'll think, 'Lord, the shoals are out at the cape,' and I'd love to be there. Oh, I loved to prowl the shoals. But I'll just have to get out of that."

Toby Sugg
Carnival Man

The tax man stood in the doorway, a gray man carrying a receipt pad. Toby Sugg looked up from his chair built on a grocery cart base and eyed him warily.

"How much?" Toby asked.

"Three hundred."

Toby shook his head with a look of disgust. He started telling about expenses, about how he had only one truck running and how the rain had wiped out business all week.

"I grossed $25 last night," he said.

The tax man showed no sign of mercy. "Well, you're making a lot of money, aren't you?"

"Shit!" said Toby, reaching for his checkbook.

And with that he commenced cursing "thievin' politicians" with such style and fervor it was a shame there was no politician there to hear it, for the poor tax man could never hope to relay the real spirit of the occasion.

"We'll see you next trip," the tax man said, smiling weakly, pocketing the check, obviously relieved to be leaving.

"If you miss me one or two times now, I won't say nothin' about it," Toby called after him. "Yeah," he said, turning back to me. "They get me every way I go."

Toby Sugg is a carnival man. From late February until December, he is on the road, playing shopping centers, community celebrations, small fairs in towns all across North Carolina, only occasionally dipping into South Carolina and Virginia. That $300 he gave the tax man is the price he must pay the State of North Carolina each week for the privilege of setting up his carnival.

That is just the beginning. City and county licenses usually cost as much as $175 a week. Insurance is sky high. And the state extracts another $10 a week as a ride inspection fee.

"And they don't know nothin' about them rides," Toby said, still fuming. "Things that'll kill somebody they don't even know . . ."

Toby is still mad about his ferris wheel. The state won't let him use it unless he has it X-rayed for structural defects. The trouble is, Toby can't find an X-ray clinic that takes in ferris wheels. He

40

offered to load the wheel with double its maximum load for a test, but the state said no. A carnival without a ferris wheel. Toby shook his head.

Do not feel sorry for Toby before considering he drives a new red and white Cadillac and owns large amounts of property. Not all of that came from shopping center carnivals, however.

Toby is 37 now. He was born with dwarfed legs that curl beneath him so he appears to have no legs at all. He gets around his small midway in a golf cart. In his trailer, there is his chair built on a grocery cart base. When he has to, he walks on his hands.

Toby was reared on an eastern North Carolina farm by his grandfather, who died when Toby was 14. Left alone, he decided to make it on his own. He chose the only way he knew: gambling. He had learned all about cards and dice from the field hands on the farm. He soon was going where the big money was, and he was doing very well for himself.

"I bought a couple of horses, bought a new Cadillac convertible, had money in my pocket all the time. I sent a brother through college; he's a doctor now. I quit school in the sixth grade."

At a bust-out crap game in a Wilmington motel, Toby met a carnival manager. "I won a bunch of money off of him a couple of times. He kept telling me about his carnival. I decided to give it a try."

He started operating a dice table on his friend's midway. "I worked for him one week and I seen how strong the money was, so I just went out and built my own table."

He hooked up with other carnivals for a while, then bought himself an evangelist's big tent and started traveling up and down the interstate highways, setting up on the edges of towns with a girly show and game booths. He did that for nearly 10 years, until it quit paying as well as he thought it should (too many thievin' politicians with their hands out, Toby says). Three years earlier, he had moved into the more sedate life of the shopping center carnival. Without a ferris wheel.

A Scrambler, he has. A Bullet. A few kiddie rides. A fun house. And the game booths, of course. Much tamer than those he once operated . . . toss a ball, grab a plastic duck.

"I don't want to see nobody come out here and lose all the money they got; more carnivals have lost more shopping centers for that reason alone than for any other. If you get two or three dollars from every person, you can make a living. I try to let everybody leave here happy. Now them ol' cotton field carnivals,

41

they wasn't that way."

Wilson last week, Hickory next, the tax man waiting at every stop. Lots of headaches. Equipment breaking down. Trying to hire people to work.

"You can't get no help. Nobody wants to work. They got too many giveaway programs. Winos come out till they get enough to get a bottle of wine, then they want to quit."

Just as Toby started talking about the low quality of the help he does get, a young man, one of his game operators, appeared at the ticket window built into the end of his trailer.

"Just like that one right there," Toby said loudly. "He ain't worth a shit for nothin'!"

He flung open the window.

"I got a beef today where you beat a kid for $20 and a pocketknife," he said angrily.

The way Toby lit into cursing him, you'd have thought the guy was a politician. The young man started trying to make excuses.

"I don't like alibis around, or alibi coots!" Toby shouted. "Now get out of my face!"

Not exactly an easy life, is it? I said.

"It's whatever you get used to," Toby said, settling back. "This is the only thing I know. I been on the road since I was 14. I ain't never knowed no other kind of life."

September, 1977
Goldsboro, North Carolina

42

Dallis Rose
Clammer

Dallis Rose had spent the morning working at the church, helping to get ready for the big camp meeting that was coming up.

He worked right through lunch, because he didn't want to quit until the job was done, and by the time he got home to eat, splattered with white paint, it was well after two and too late to go fishing. He'd heard that some of the boys had been picking up Spanish mackerel off Cape Lookout, and he thought he might be able to get a load before the afternoon was gone.

Instead, he decided to go clamming.

This was Monday, and he had clammed on Thursday and Friday the week before, taking about eight bushels for the two days' work, a good take nowadays. He expected no such luck this day. Not with this late start.

He might not have gone at all, but it was so hot he really wanted to get into the water.

"I reckon I sweat more than anybody in the world," he said. "That's why I like to get in the water. Lot of people don't like the water like I do. I'm like a duck. I just like to be in the water and around the water."

And, too, he needed clams for the chowder that would be made and served at the camp meeting.

But it was after three by the time he'd finished eating and got down to the docks where his boat was tied. He built the boat himself, a sturdy, 28-foot wooden boat that he used for netting fish and shrimp. As soon as he opened the cabin, he saw he'd had unwelcome visitors over the weekend.

Drunks sometimes crawled into his boat to sleep on his cot and drink his instant coffee. There wasn't much he could do about it. This time one had left the electric lightbulb burning and when Dallis Rose tried the engine, the battery, as he suspected, was dead. He had to take the battery from his truck to get the boat going, causing even further delay.

By the time he finally got the boat out of the harbor and into the channel headed toward the lighthouse at Cape Lookout, towing a skiff behind, the tide was very low, so low, he feared, that he would not be able to get to the best clamming grounds.

He climbed through the hatch and sat atop the cabin, where he

43

could feel the cooling breeze. He steered with his stockinged foot and talked of clamming.

"It's been a lifetime work with me," he said. "I wouldn't be satisfied doing anything else. I was born and raised in it. It's not a popular job, because you're crawling around in the mud most of the time. I couldn't say it hasn't been a good life, though."

Dallis Rose has been a clammer for more than 50 years. He was born and reared on Harker's Island, and he began gathering clams as a child. He started working at it regularly when he was about 12, as best he can recall. He is 63 now, and he is not as robust as he once was.

"My health and age is against me now."

He'd had some heart trouble and arthritis bothered his arms a lot. Sometimes his arms would just give way when he tried to lift the heavy buckets of clams.

"A few years ago," he was saying, "I didn't stop for the tide. I'd work right on through and that's one reason I caught a lot of clams. I've seen the day when I'd be out here long before anybody else got here, and I'd be here hours after they'd gone. They used to kid me and tell me they were going to have to copper my bottom, I stayed out here so much.

"I don't even hardly try to keep up now. I used to average about five bushels a day. I have caught as high as 13, 14 bushels in one day. That's a few years ago, when I was younger. If we could have got the price then that we do now, I could've made some money."

The price the clammers get now is four cents each for the small clams that end up steamed or served raw on the half shell in northern restaurants, four cents a pound for the big tough ones that must be minced for chowder, and a bushel of good clams can bring $20 or more.

Dallis Rose laughed.

"Back in the Depression, I caught clams for 30 cents a bushel. Sometimes you couldn't even get that on Harker's Island. We'd take 'em to the store and trade 'em.

"In those days, you could go about anywhere you wanted to and catch some clams. Now that bottom out there, most places, you couldn't catch a dozen clams in hours."

Years earlier, he had seen the big boats come with their sand blowers and dredges, methodically vacuuming the bottom until most of the clams were gone. Now the clams are only in certain areas, and they are widespread, seldom more than three or four in a spot.

"It's been clammed so much," Dallis Rose said. "There's just a little patch here and a little patch there." He grinned. "We call 'em Indian clams — a little Apache here, a little Apache there."

Most of the clammers gather them the way Dallis Rose does, the old way, crawling through the water, feeling through the mud for them with hands and feet.

" 'Nother words," he was saying, "the Lord knew how to fix it so nobody could get 'em all. The amount of effort you put out is what you get. That's the way clamming is. It's about like piecework."

He had left the channel now and slowed the boat as he headed across the shallow flats toward the distant clamming grounds. The tide was so low the bottom scraped several times.

"We may not be able to get to where they're really catching clams," he said.

He pointed to a distant grouping of boats.

"That's the clammers in there now. Four boats, maybe a dozen people in there now. No, wait, there's some other boats. There's another gang up in there."

One of the boats he recognized as his son's.

The water had grown too shallow for the big boat to continue. "We'll have to stop and take the skiff," he said.

He poled the skiff to a group of tiny, grassy islands, some distance from the other clammers, before he climbed into the water, pulled on a pair of rubber gloves and a floppy old hat, attached a big, truck-tire inner tube supporting a washtub to his belt with a rope and set to work, crawling through the shallow water, feeling through the grassy bottom for clams.

"Sure feels good to be in this water," he said, "but you can see why it's not a popular job."

He brought to the surface an urchin with long, sharp spines. "Lot of things out here that can hurt you."

In addition to the urchins (the clammers call them porcupines), there are sharp shells, toadfish that bite ferociously, and other hazards. "It can be hard on your hands," he said, grinning.

Whenever he came too close to the small islands, the terns rose, hovering and diving over him, screeching angrily. He tried to soothe them. "No, we're not going to hurt your babies. See, the seaweed washes up there, and they just lay their eggs in it."

The big tub he pulled behind him was filling slowly. "They're scarce," he said. "These used to be good grounds, but they've just been picked over too many times."

It was almost sundown and the other clammers had all

45

departed on the fast-rising tide when Dallis Rose finally finished filling the tub and began dumping his clams into the skiff to make his way back to the boat. His catch was only about two bushels, hardly worth the effort of coming out.

"You might as well say that clamming is a thing of the past," he said. "Well, we'll go home now — if our motor will start."

July, 1976
Harker's Island, North Carolina

Captain Sinbad
Pirate

The day Captain Sinbad and his band of rogues attacked the famous Sanitary Fish Market Restaurant on the Morehead City waterfront, the customers loved it. But the management was a little upset.

The attack came at noon on Sunday, one of the restaurant's busiest times, and the rogues spirited away four waitresses as hostages.

"They didn't think it was a bit funny," Captain Sinbad is saying of the management, still a bit puzzled over their reaction.

The Coast Guard didn't think it was funny either when one of its cutters was attacked near Norfolk by an 18th-century brigantine with Jolly Roger flying, cannon blasting and wild-looking characters lobbing water balloons. The cutter captain issued an all-hands alert, and the would-be boarders were repelled with fire hoses.

"They just killed us," says Sinbad. "Got our powder all wet. We were hiding, begging for mercy . . ."

It's not easy being a pirate nowadays. Sinbad can testify to that. The wonder, of course, is that it is possible to be a pirate at all, but somehow, despite everything, he has managed.

A few years back, when lots of people were telling him that someday he'd have to grow up and quit playing pirate, he always had a one-word question for them: Why?

Since nobody could give him a good answer, he didn't see why he couldn't and shouldn't become a pirate. Looking back, he can see that even as a child playing pirate on the Rocky River in northeastern Ohio, he knew that was what he would become. He realized even then that although he had never seen it, the sea was a part of him.

At age 11, he built his first boat, an eight-foot sailing pram. His family had moved to Detroit, where his father worked as an engineer, and he sailed his boat on the Great Lakes. He later advanced to speed boats and discovered they really weren't his speed. He preferred the days of yore, when vessels moved under the wind.

By then he had discovered C.S. Forester's *Horatio Hornblower*. He read those books voraciously, and for a while he thought he wanted to be Hornblower (and now and then he is), but piracy had first call.

At 16, bored with school, he dropped out and ran away from home. "I just didn't like school," he recalls. "I never did like our way of education. And I had this intense interest in sailing. I was just eager to get going on these things."

He made his way to the West Indies, where he found work on charter sailing ships and became Captain Sinbad. The native crew members called him that because they had trouble pronouncing his legal name, Ross Morphew, a name he rarely uses anymore.

His father eventually convinced him to return home and finish high school, and after Sinbad's graduation, his father tried to talk him into going on to college to study engineering. "I had leanings toward it," Sinbad recalls, "but it just wasn't in my blood. I knew that I wanted my own boat. I wanted to go exploring. I wanted to see the world. I wasn't about to stay in one spot."

He set to work building himself another boat, a 22-foot midget ocean sloop. When it was finished, he took a mate, and he and his bride, Marilyn, set sail through the Saint Lawrence Seaway to the West Indies, where they hoped to take up the charter trade They had named their vessel *Meka*, the phonetic spelling of a Hopi Indian word meaning stout, loyal companion. Three days out of New York, 200 miles off Cape Hatteras, the *Meka* proved to be not quite so stout and loyal. She broke up and sank in rough seas whipped up by Hurricane Donna. Sinbad and his bride clung to a life raft for six hours before being rescued by a passing freighter and deposited in Norfolk.

They flew back home to Detroit minus belongings, including their wedding gifts, and a short time later flew to the West Indies on borrowed money. Six months was all they needed to know the charter business wasn't for them. They wanted a family, and the business wasn't conducive to family living.

For a while, it might have seemed that Sinbad had become a typical middle-class suburbanite. He took a job as layout draftsman for General Motors back in Detroit. He and Marilyn moved into a rented house in suburban Dearborn Heights and started a family. But all the time, Sinbad was planning. He was going to build another boat.

"I wanted an old-time vessel. I'm extremely interested in naval history, especially pirates, privateers. I wanted a vessel I could build and try to live the part. I wanted a strong, livable home, because I knew I was going to be living on it the rest of my life."

He settled on a brigantine, a ship used extensively in American trade in the 1700s, and in 1965 he set to work building one in his backyard. The boat took all his free time and money, and at one point he had loans from five different banks. As the vessel took shape, problems developed. Neighbors complained, and Sinbad, the pirate, had to fight his first big battle to be able to build his ship in his own back yard. He lost, and in 1967, in a blatant case of discrimination against pirates, he was evicted from Dearborn Heights. His ship was still only a shell, and he had to sell most of his belongings just to get it deposited in Lake Erie.

Problems also developed with his job. He had taken all his vacation, holidays, even a leave of absence. The ship and the fight to build it had consumed all his energies. "I was frazzled," he says. His bosses called him in and told him he had a bright future at General Motors, but he couldn't keep playing pirate. He had to make a choice. For Sinbad, of course, there was no choice.

"The boat was in the water; the sea was calling. There was no way that I could possibly be landlocked in a fluorescent lighted drafting room for the rest of my life."

He and his family moved into their shell of a ship and set to work completing it. Sinbad found work with a construction company and a shipyard to keep going. By 1970 the vessel was seaworthy. They named it *Meka II* and set sail for warmer waters. This time as they headed south, they took the inland route around Hatteras.

For three years, they sailed Florida waters, and their fourth child ("We call them crew.") was born there. Sinbad had thought he might make his way as a film maker. When that didn't work out, he took work repairing other peoples' boats. One of those jobs brought him to North Carolina in 1973.

The owner of a 72-foot trawler Sinbad was rebuilding was erecting a house near Morehead City and wanted to bring the boat north. He asked Sinbad to come and finish the work. Sinbad and family sailed north in the *Meka II*, planning to stay only three months. But once in these waters where Blackbeard and other pirates had sailed, Sinbad knew he was home. "We kind of fell in love with it," he says.

He set up a repair shop at Spooner's Creek and went about doing the things pirates have always done — raiding vessels and land posts, spiriting away maidens, having a good time.

"Last year I was a privateer," he says. "I was sort of a gentleman pirate." He did that in honor of the bicentennial, but now he has returned to being a rogue. "It's more lucrative and a lot more fun anyways."

Just Folks

He is sitting on the dock beside his ship on the waterfront at Beaufort, where he recently established a pirate's den. He has moved his repair shop here and changed the registry of the *Meka II*, on which he and his family still live in crowded harmony, to Beaufort. His hair is long and tied back. He wears a bandana around his head, pirate-style. A tiny gold ring dangles from his left ear. It is his everyday dress. At 33, Sinbad is still playing pirate and has no plans ever to quit. He is talking about some of his recent raids.

"We attacked two vessels up at Ocracoke. We had a really good fight up there. We get into some horrible water balloon fights."

Nobody in or near North Carolina waters is really safe from attack by Captain Sinbad. He usually swoops down without warning. Two days before, he had attacked the town of Beaufort and been repelled by cannon fire and musketry. The town was ready for him because he attacks every year on the same date to commemorate the anniversary of the town's invasion by real pirates.

Sinbad even attacked a Russian ship (along with a lot of others), when he and his wife (who has taken to calling herself Lieutenant Bush, after Horatio Hornblower's sidekick) sailed with their crew to New York to enliven the parade of tall ships that was one of the highlights of the nation's bicentennial celebration.

"We've attacked *hundreds* of vessels," he says proudly. And seldom does anybody take the attack in any spirit but fun. Even the Russians seemed to enjoy it. Only one group looks askance at the whole business.

"The U.S. Coast Guard always gives you the hard time," Sinbad says. "They're just absolutely *stodgy*."

July, 1977
Beaufort, North Carolina

Winkley Locklear
Banking in the Smokehouse

The house was set back far from the road, as most of the old houses are. It was roofed with tin and never painted and it has grayed with the years. Even though it was a winter day the doors stood open.

No grass grew around the house. The yard was hard-packed soil. Bushes crowded the front porch, and at the sides and back of the house bare-limbed pecan trees swayed with the wind. The trees didn't bear this year.

The corncrib, smokehouse and mule barn stood in a row not far from the house, forming the remainder of the man-made island in the open reaches of rich, flat fields.

Winkley Locklear was raking leaves under his pecan trees. Seventy-eight years old, he is not a big man. His face is drawn, weathered like his house, his features distinctly Indian, his hair snowy white. He was wearing an old hat, overalls, a heavy jacket and work gloves.

When the callers drove up, Winkley Locklear put down his rake and came over to the car. One of the callers was Adolph Dial, a history professor at Pembroke State University. Dial was born and reared in this community, called Prospect, near Pembroke, where all the land is owned by Lumbee Indians. Winkley Locklear didn't recognize Dial immediately, and Dial had to explain who he was, talking loudly because Mr. Winkley, as many of his neighbors call him, doesn't hear so well anymore. When he finally recognized Dial, Mr. Winkley called his sister from the house. "Hey, Nancy, come here."

His sister, a tiny, bent woman with a deeply lined face, came from the house bundled in heavy clothing, wearing a bonnet. She is 80. "You'll have to speak up," Mr. Winkley said confidentially. "She can't hear too good."

It was all explained again about who Adolph Dial was, and then there was much talk about whose boy was whose, and whose brother and sister was whose, and where this one was and that one is, a great passing of family information.

Then Mr. Winkley got to the point. "What you selling?" he asked.

"We're not selling anything," said Dial. "We're just visiting."

51

"Why, get out and set awhile," said Mr. Winkley. "I thought you was selling something."

We got out.

"Your people been on this land back on this swamp a long time, haven't they?" said Dial.

"Oh, yeah," said Mr. Winkley. He led us into the house to a fireplace. He had something to show us. On the mantle was a picture of a tall man and a short woman, the picture veiled with wispy white cloth. "That's my mother and father," he said.

We returned to the wide back porch then and sat on rope-bottomed chairs and talked. Battered washpans hung on the walls above a crude table bearing water buckets and dippers. A Dr. Pepper thermometer hung by the door. There was more talk about family and preachers and other folk. Adolph Dial said he was working at the college, was planning to write a book about the Lumbee people. Mr. Winkley propped his feet on the porch railing and looked at him.

"You just make a world of money, don't you?" he said.

Dial laughed. "Money will make you unhappy, didn't you know that?"

"I don't know whether it would or not. Depends on how you use it."

"You never worried about a dollar, did you?" said Dial.

"I always took care of my business."

A passerby, not knowing, might look at Winkley Locklear and his place and think he was among the poverty stricken. That would be a mistake. Mr. Winkley simply prefers the old ways. He did recently make a concession and have an indoor toilet installed, just for the convenience, and because he and Miz Nancy aren't getting any younger. But he doesn't think much of it.

He acknowledges he is doing okay. He has his land, 100 acres in this tract, another 160 acres over toward the swamp, half of which he is selling to a son-in-law. He sharecrops his land, gets his cut. His corncrib is full. "God, I've got corn. I shelled up 200 bushels. I've got that barn chock full. I got that mule barn as full as I can get it. I've got more than 1,000 bushels. Oh, yes, good Lord, I've got a world of corn."

The smokehouse, too, is packed. "I just killed about two weeks ago. I killed three hogs. I give a lot of it away. We don't eat it all. I give it away." And his collard patch is still producing. "I love my collards better than anything," he says.

Mr. Winkley, indeed, is doing so well that he is a mark for robbers. "I've been robbed twice. They got $5,000 the first time." They got that from the smokehouse where he had hidden it in a Mason jar. The second time the thieves got only $200. They got that from the smokehouse, too. Mr. Winkley shook his head. "I just had to quit keeping any money out there," he said.

Mr. Winkley has spent all but a little of his life on his land. "I was in War One," he said. "We Indian boys when we was in the war had a good time. I wanted to go across. I'd a loved to a-went across." He didn't go overseas, though. He came back to his land and raised his children. Four are still living. His wife died 20 years ago. Now just he and his sister remain on the place.

Adolph Dial asked him how things were different, when he was a younger man. "I tell you the truth, it's a world of difference," he replied. "When I was a young man, it was a good time. But it's not now. No, good gracious . . . people's a lot different than they was. They don't love one another. They don't visit one another like they did. Used to be they'd holp one another. They'd give to one another. Somebody got sick, they'd visit, holp 'em along. People don't give to one another now. Everybody's looking after theirself. It's terrible now."

A group of pigs wandered snorting across the yard, two dogs chasing after the younger ones, nipping at their heels. A mule-drawn wagon creaked along a rutted road in the distance. The subject turned to other things, more pleasant things, hunting and fishing.

"Lord, yes," Mr. Winkley said, "I fished a lot when I was a boy. I ain't been a-fishin' in 30 years, I reckon. I used to fish, but I used to be awful to hunt. Good gracious, I loved to hunt. I had all my dogs. I kept my dogs. I only got those two now. They ain't huntin' dogs. I don't hunt no more."

Miz Nancy, as she is usually called, sat listening to all this without saying much. "You still like your snuff?" Dial asked. She smiled, embarrassed, covered her mouth with her hand and nodded. "I saw you get a little dip of that snuff," he kidded.

The conversation continued with Dial recalling the story about the time Abner Locklear's body was being sent back from the war. A mournful crowd had gathered at the train station. The train pulled up and here came Abner climbing down from one of the cars. People rushed to him. "We thought you were dead, Abner," somebody said. "Well, I'm sorry y'all got disappointed," he drawled. Dial was laughing. "You remember that?"

"Yeah, I remember that good."

Somehow, that led to talk of the government and government programs. Dial asked Mr. Winkley what he thought about Social Security. Mr. Winkley scratched his head. "I reckon it's all right," he said. "I don't know. The government'll get that money back somehow, though. Government don't give you nothing."

Dial laughed. "I declare, Mr. Winkley," he said, "you're really a mess . . ."

January, 1971
Pembroke, North Carolina

The Haul Seiner

For more than a month he had been watching the ocean, going down to the beach every morning before dawn and staying until well after nightfall. But still the fish hadn't come.

"They're usually in the water by now," he said, "but they ain't even caught none in Virginia or North Carolina yet from what I hear. Might be on account of that pollution. That's all I can figure . . . I don't know what it is. Maybe them Russian folks is catching all of 'em out there. All I know, there ain't been no fish going through here."

It had not always been that way. In the 40 years he had been setting nets in the surf, always at this same spot on the southern end of Myrtle Beach, once an isolated spot, now in the shadows of high-rise motels, he had seen and caught a lot of fish.

"I've stood here and watched 'em going by out yonder in rafts for a month at a time, steady going. Right on the high rise out yonder. See the sharks cutting through 'em. Cutting 'em up. Just rafts of 'em. A month at a time. Hell, yes, there used to be more fish."

Year after year, he watched the numbers decline, the catch grow smaller. There was nothing he could do about it. The state cut the season and allowed him only three months — September, October, November — to make his annual catch. And the migrating fish had to escape a lot of other nets up the coast before they got to him on their fall runs southward.

"There's four or five hundred nets along the line. Up in Virginia and North Carolina. Fifteen up here at Ocean Drive and Cherry Grove. I'm the last man on the run."

The fish he watched for were spots and mullet. He hated the bluefish and sharks that oftentimes fed in the schools and ripped his nets to shreds. He preferred catching spots. They were easier to sell and brought a higher price. Mullet were becoming harder and harder to sell. So far this season he had caught only mullet. "I caught about 30 boxes here a week ago, but that's all I've done all fall until yesterday."

The day before he had made two good catches, one in the morning, another late in the afternoon. He figured he'd caught maybe three tons of mullet, although he hadn't bothered to weigh them. The fish rested now in two old trucks that dripped with melting ice.

55

"They ain't nowhere to take 'em," he said with resignation. "If I got a sale of 'em, I'd take 'em, but don't nobody want 'em. Used to be, years ago, you could sell 'em, but there just ain't no market no more. I bury most of 'em the way it's been happening."

Even though the fish were stacked up, unable to be sold, he knew that if the weather were right and the fish were out there, he would have been out there on this day, too, driven by instinct, catching even more. "I was born up with it," he said. "They's been a fishery here since . . . oh, my granddaddy run one here before I was born, I reckon."

He had tried other types of fishing in his life, but he didn't care for them. As a boy, he went out on the boats. "I quit that," he says. "I don't go out there. I just got to where I didn't care nothing about going out there." Netting in the surf, haul seining, it is called, just somehow seemed the only way to fish.

It was never easy work. The net, 200 yards long, had to be taken out through the surf in a small boat, then pulled in by hand. Farther up the coast, haul seiners used tractors to bring the nets in, but the slope of the beach was too great here to allow the use of tractors. Usually it took 12 or 15 men to haul in the net, mostly old black men who had worked with him for years on shares. But there had been many times when he had to beg help from bystanders to keep from losing a catch.

In all his years of fishing he had developed a theory about the habits of fish and what causes them to act so strangely at times. "Fish works just like anything else," he said. "They work with the moon. Just like women. Every time the moon changes, they swell up, puff up, and raise hell. That's right. That's the way they are. They just like a woman. They ornery as hell."

He was sitting on a fish box as he talked, looking out at the waves pounding the beach and the white caps kicked up by the wind beyond. With the weather against him, he had spent this day mending his net (Sharks had been in his last catch the day before. He and his men had clubbed a 10-footer to death, but others had ripped big holes.) and selling mullet three pounds for a dollar to people who came to buy a dollar's worth or two.

"No," he said, "I don't even break even some years. My wife gives me hell every night because of this damn stuff. Hell, I don't get home 'til about nine or 10 o'clock at night, get up before day in the morning. It's hell, I tell you that. But it's something I just love to do, and I've stuck at it. I've not got enough of it yet."

October, 1976
Myrtle Beach, South Carolina

David Marshall Williams
Carbine Inventor

Just down the road from J.V. Tew's store, at a cluster of five tall pines, a rutted sand road juts off through the fields. It leads to Carbine's place.

The house is small and white with a tin roof, a picket fence and a yardful of chinaberry, pecan and magnolia trees. Cool, green, quiet. Potato fields stretch away front and side. The house was once a tenant farmer's on the Williams' spread.

Carbine Williams is waiting. He is suspicious of strangers. "I pay attention to my surroundings," he puts it. An old moonshiner's trait. Short and stout, he wears Lee overalls, a gray work shirt and combat boots. His once red sideburns flare white. His eyes are pale blue and piercing. His brow is furrowed deeply, like the potato fields. He looks not unlike many another Cumberland County farmer.

The white Stetson hat gives the only hint that David Marshall Williams was ever anything other than a Cumberland County farmer. It was made specially for him. It cost $100.

The hat goes back to the days when Carbine Williams wore double-breasted, pin-striped suits, a ruby-encrusted belt buckle and pearl-handled revolvers. He was rich and flamboyant. He owned hotels and nightclubs, a big mansion up north, and a vitamin factory. He carried diamonds in his pocket like marbles.

The story is told that Carbine was strolling along Fifth Avenue in New York one day when a huge emerald-cut diamond in one of the fancy jewelry stores caught his eye.

"How much?" Carbine asked the stuffy salesman, who looked down his nose and sniffed: "Forty-four thousand."

From a roll in his pocket, Carbine peeled off forty-four 1,000-dollar bills, tossed them onto the counter and dropped the diamond into his pocket.

Those were the high times.

That was when a big Hollywood movie was made about Carbine's life. Jimmy Stewart played Carbine. The movie made his story familiar all over the country.

He was a country boy wanting to get ahead. He got into the bootlegging business. It was an accepted thing in this part of the country. There was a raid. A gunfight. A deputy sheriff was killed. And Marshall Williams went to prison for murder. While he was in prison, with the warden's approval, he designed and developed a gun that was to revolutionize the manufacture of automatic weapons. After 11 years in prison, he was pardoned. Many gun patents followed, but it was the carbine he developed in prison that made him rich and famous. Eight million of those were manufactured during World War II.

But that is past . . .

It has been 15 years since Carbine Williams brought out a new gun. Troubled years. His riches and all the trappings are gone now, but he is at work again. The Army is looking at a new machine gun he has invented . . .

Carbine calls his dog Spot, and the dog bounds from beneath a shed at the back of the house and hops into the car for the short trip through the pines to the gun shop.

"Been foolin' 'round this morning, ain't got to feeling right yet," Carbine says. "Seems like today ain't been a smooth day for some reason or t'other."

It is mid-afternoon and well into the day for Carbine. He rises early. "I just use farmer's hours, you know. I wouldn't want to be laying around the house with everybody else at work."

The gun shop is a small white building with peeling paint and a padlock on the door. It looks like a one-room country schoolhouse. The gun shop stands near the site of the old Williams homeplace. The house is gone now, but the boxwoods have grown tall, and the mulberry trees where General Sherman's men were said to have once tied their horses still bloom. There is a well with a hand pump nearby and the water is cold and sweet. "Mighty good water if you like water," says Carbine. "Some people don't. You can't get enough of that yonder."

Inside, the air is hot and stale. Fat green horseflies buzz in the windows. The room is neat and in perfect order. Every tool has its place. A pot-bellied stove squats in the middle of the floor. Robert E. Lee looks down from the wall. A shaggy buffalo head with dusty hair adorns one wall with help from the tops of two deer. Carbine shot the buffalo in Wyoming.

Over a work bench hang a framed copy of Kipling's "If," Carbine's favorite poem; an old saying, "Fate makes our relatives, choice makes our friends;" and a clipping from a man-on-the-street interview in the *New York Daily Mirror*: Question — "Should the atom bomb be used to shorten the Korean War?" Carbine's answer — "Not only should we use the atom bomb but any other weapon our government has to shorten the Korean War."

Carbine spends a lot of time in the gun shop, spewing curse

words when things don't go right. He fixes a small target in a bank outside, comes back, props a carbine in the window and squeezes off three shots. They are center target. You could cover the holes with a dime.

Carbine isn't much of a talker. "Don't hardly know what the hell to talk to you about," he says. Though sometimes he talks about the past. "They had a guv'n'ment still here in the old days," he recalls with a little smile. "I remember going there bigger'n hell."

It is cooler outside and the well water is refreshing. Carbine looks over the site where the old homeplace stood. He had planned to build a big new house there. He just never did. His brother plows nearby. It stirs Carbine's memory.

"Long time ago, some of us boys was having a contest who could grow the most corn in Cumberland County," he says. "Damn, I won it. I forget how much we raised. Considerable over 100 bushels. Put it in that old barn over there . . ."

Carbine is quiet on the trip back to the house. Maggie, his wife, comes out to say goodbye. She had a heart attack a while back and can't move around much. Carbine shakes his head as he stands beside the car.

"Seems like today things is working on a rusty hinge somehow. Maybe not . . ."

August, 1968
Godwin, North Carolina

In 1971, Carbine Williams donated many of his guns, as well as his gunshop, to the State of North Carolina. His gunshop was recreated in the North Carolina Museum of History in Raleigh. Carbine died January 8, 1975. Shortly before his death, he was still trying to sell rights to a new rapid-fire lightweight machine gun he had invented.

George Lockhart
Shark Man

You are most likely to see him in late afternoon. He will be wearing his flat seaman's cap, and his beard will be flowing in the breeze as he pedals his three-wheeled bike toward the waterfront where the fishing boats dock.

His tackle box will be in the basket between the rear wheels. Two huge rods with massive reels will be sticking up in back like radio antennas. As he wheels past the docks, he will hear the calls of greeting, "Hey, Shark Man!"

"Nobody on the waterfront knows my whole name," George Lockhart says. "They just call me Shark Man."

He's grown to prefer it.

It is a rare night that does not find Shark Man fishing for sharks, usually off the waterfront docks, but sometimes off the rocks at Fort Macon or in the sound off Shackleford Banks, even in the surf at Atlantic Beach.

"Sharks," says Shark Man with great respect, "I call 'em poor man's marlin."

Shark Man's fascination with sharks is total. When he is not fishing for them, he is reading about them, cleaning, preserving, mounting their jaws, mining their fossilized teeth in a quarry near New Bern. He has found some monstrous teeth big enough, he believes, to have come from sharks more than 100 feet long.

Shark Man was 15 when he hooked his first shark. He and his mother were fishing for king mackerel off a pier at Atlantic Beach when a shark took his line.

"My Mom came running, yelling, 'Cut the line! Cut the line!'" he recalls. "I said, 'No way. I'm going to get 'im.'"

He got him, too, a four-and-a-half-foot hammerhead. "We started shark fishing all the time then," he remembers. When he was 16, he found a woman's wristwatch in the belly of a big shark he landed.

But George Lockhart wasn't to become Shark Man until eight years later in 1972. He'd suffered a nervous breakdown in the Army and began having epileptic seizures after his discharge. He found it difficult to hold a job. His thoughts returned to the shark fishing he'd enjoyed so much before joining the Army.

"I knew I had to find something to do to at least hold my time.

61

Just Folks

So I said, 'That's what I'll do. I'll go fishing.' I just started fishing for sharks."

He has no idea how many he has caught since then. Hundreds. Some very large ones. He has pictures of most of those.

"This one here was caught in the surf," he says, passing me the picture. "It was nine and a half feet. I caught 15 in one night. That's four I brought home."

The thrill of hooking a shark is as great to him now as it was when he caught that first one 16 years ago. He knows that other people feel the excitement too, even if they've never caught a fish.

"There could be nobody around, and if you hook one, there'll be 500 people around you; you can't hardly step back. Everybody is attracted to that unknown thing. You don't know what it is. It might not even be a shark. It might be a stingray. It might be a piece of lumber drifting by. I hooked and brought up a shovel one day. I thought I had something."

The shovel isn't mounted on the wall of his small house, but lots of shark jaws are.

"This is a tiger," he says, pointing to a large set of jaws, "and he'd eaten this small dusky shark, so I just mounted both of 'em together. This was a ten-and-a-half-foot lemon shark."

Cabinets are filled with shark teeth. "People call all the time, say,'Shark Man, you got any shark's teeth for sale, or jaws?' I say, 'How many you want and what size?' "

He also mounts jaws of sharks caught by others, and someday he hopes to become a guide for people who want to fish for sharks, although he has no boat. Sharks, he says, are plentiful in all of the Carolinas' coastal waters. He has seen schools of black tips churning the water in feeding frenzies.

Why, I ask, are not more people attacked by sharks?

"There's enough of their normal diet here for 'em not to bother people," he tells me. "But if their food supply was to diminish, you can bet your life they'd be in the surf attacking people."

If any shark ever attacks Shark Man, it'll have to come out of the water or pull him in to do it. "No sir," he says emphatically, "I don't go swimming at all."

August, 1979
Morehead City, North Carolina

Joe Rock
King of Marathon Dancers

The first call comes just before midnight from a big guy sitting at the back of the bar.

"Don't Cry Joe!" he yells over the din of the crowded room.

"*What?*" says his female companion, an obvious newcomer.

"Get Don't Cry Joe to sing," he explains.

Within minutes, Randy Owen, lead singer of a country-rock band called Alabama, is telling the crowd that this is a very special occasion, an anniversary. On this night, July 4, 1978, Don't Cry Joe has been bartender at the Bowery, Myrtle Beach's oldest and most famous bar, for 32 years.

"Here he is," says Owen, "*Don't Cry Joe!*"

Don't Cry Joe makes his way to the stage with a gap-toothed grin. He wears a gaudy, flowered sportshirt and gaudy frayed Bermuda shorts. His crewcut is white now and he walks a little stiffly, slightly bent. He takes the microphone and immediately begins to sing "Your Cheatin' Heart."

"*All right!*" yells the big guy at the bar, applauding loudly.

Bugs Schronce, manager of the Bowery, shakes his head. "Goina have to cut Charlie off back there," he says.

At first the crowd seems not to know quite what to make of this old man in funny clothes as he strays ahead, then lags behind the band. It is mostly a young crowd, and most of them, no doubt, never heard of Don't Cry Joe. But they begin to warm to him as he brazenly forges on into his mournful theme song, "Don't Cry Joe." And by the time he takes a sprightly step into a belligerent rendition of "It's a Long Way to Tipperary," they are whooping and hollering, and Don't Cry Joe leaves the bandstand to cheers.

"I'm no singer," he says, somewhat unnecessarily, "but I try it. I can't sing. Hell, I wish I could."

But singing was never his line. No, dancing was what appealed to Don't Cry Joe. And he was very good at it. He once was called Joe Rock. He danced with his sister, Mary. They were, he claims, the king and queen of marathon dancers, reigning in the '30s when dance marathons were epidemic across the land. Nobody ever topped their record.

Around the corner from the Bowery, at Ripley's Believe It or Not Museum, visitors can learn all about how in 1933 at Madison

63

Square Garden, Joe and Mary Rock danced for 5,295 hours, taking only a 15-minute break every hour.

"Seven months and 10 days," Joe says.

"What did you do when it was over?" I ask.

Joe laughs. "Slept four hours and went to a dance the next night. It's no lie! You don't believe it, do you?"

Joe was 19 when he and his sister entered their first marathon in Chicago in 1927. The promoter got the idea for the marathon from the popular six-day bicycle races. This was a six-day dancing race with the couples dancing from pole to pole. "We beat 150 other couples by 8,000 laps," says Joe. "After that we was in the marathons all the time until the war came on and that stopped it all. It was the easiest thing in the world to do. We used to get $500 apiece for winning a show."

They won a lot of them, too, so many that they were banned from some marathons. "We were barred to dance together. We were too tough for 'em. You ought to see the damn hard dancing we used to do. I danced one show I had to carry my sister on my shoulders and I won it. I was tough when I was young."

During World War II, Joe went to work at a defense plant in New Orleans, and that was where the dancing stopped for Joe and Mary Rock. "Last marathon they had was in 1944 in the St. Charles Theater in New Orleans. We danced 1,544 hours." Two years later, Joe got a call from his sister, then living in Miami. A friend of hers, Richard Layer, was opening a bar in Myrtle Beach. Would Joe be interested in working for him? Joe started work at the Bowery on July 4, 1946. He recalls Richard Layer giving him his nickname the same day.

"When I walked in, he said, 'You want a good name?' I said, 'I don't care what you call me.' So he said, 'You'll be Don't Cry Joe,' and a year or two later it came out, the song, 'Don't Cry Joe.' "

During the intervening years, Joe has drawn a lot of beers ("Millions and millions of glasses," he says. "I can draw beer in my sleep.") and met a lot of people. Some people who drop into the bar out of nostalgia after years of absence are surprised to see Joe still at it. "Lot of people come in, say, 'Joe, I thought you'd be dead.' I say, 'I'm livin', ain't I? How can I be dead?' "

But Richard Layer is dead (the bar is operated now by Larry McDaniel) and so is Joe's sister, Mary. And Joe knows he won't be able to dance behind the bar as he draws beer much longer. "I'm 70 years old. My leg is shot. I got arthritis in my hip. Two years now. I can't dance like I used to, but I try. I do the best I can. I don't work every day no more. I just work four days a week now." He even has thought of retiring. "Well, I was goina quit this year and they asked me to come back. I don't know how my leg is going to be. If it's okay, I may work another year, what the hell."

On this night, one of the young bartenders takes a swipe at the bar with a beer-soaked towel and watches as Don't Cry Joe makes his way back to the bar after finishing his songs.

"That right there," says the young bartender, "is one hell of a dude."

July, 1978
Myrtle Beach, South Carolina

The Piedmont

Ben Owen
Master Potter

It was quite a sight when the kilns were fired. All that smoke churning up through the trees. He had two kilns out behind the log workshop, big groundhog kilns. He never switched to oil, the way most of the other potters did. He always fired with wood, the old way, the way his father did before him, and his father before him.

And what excitement it was when the kilns were opened! In all of his years at it, that was one thing Ben Owen never got over. You never knew how a piece of pottery would take the heat. There were endless surprises, some good, some bad. He always felt the excitement, like a kid with a box of Cracker Jacks, as he put it.

The smoke no longer roils from those kilns. It has been . . . what? . . . could it have been two years since he last felt that twinge of excitement on opening the kiln?

Ben Owen sits now in a rocking chair on the screened front porch of his modest white house. He lives halfway between Seagrove and Robbins on Highway 705, which once was the old plank road. A big man, Ben Owen. He has cataracts and wears thick glasses. His hair is thinning but still black, although he is now 69.

The walker, built of aluminum and plastic, stands before the chair, and Ben Owen leans forward in his gray-striped pajamas to rest his arms on it and remember . . .

"My father was a potter and so were my brothers; and my grandfather, he had a shop there in front of the home when I was a little boy, and my father turned pottery there some back in those days. But I would help my father when I was growing up, you know, a boy, fixing his clay, helping him lift his pottery off the wheel, kneading his clay for him . . ."

Because of the clay that could be found in the area, a small community of potters had settled near Seagrove as early as 1740. Ben Owen's ancestors were among them, having come from Staffordshire in England. Their pottery was plain and utilitarian: crocks, jugs, churns, bowls, dishes. Occasionally they would load their wares into covered wagons and set out to peddle them.

The Seagrove area potters were still making the same kinds of pottery when Ben turned his first pieces as a boy, practicing at the wheel after his father had finished his day's work. By age 18 he had learned the basics, and something happened that changed his life. A man named Jacques Busbee saw a pie dish Ben Owen's father had made and consequently became interested in the Seagrove area potters.

Jacques Busbee was an artist, a native of Raleigh who operated a small shop in New York. He had been commissioning potters to produce work for his shop but was dissatisfied with what he was getting. He wanted to start a pottery of his own so he could supervise the work and was thinking of getting one of the Seagrove area potters to work with him.

There was a problem. Jacques Busbee was interested in pottery for its artistic merit, as well as for its practical purposes. None of the older Seagrove area potters were interested in working with him. But Ben was young and eager to learn, and the two formed a partnership.

Jacques Busbee was not a potter, but Ben credits him with being an excellent teacher. Together they visited museums in New York, Washington, New Orleans, studying and photographing classic works from master potters throughout the world.

Jacques Busbee built his pottery in Moore County and called it Jugtown, and for 35 years Ben Owen worked there. In that time, he became one of America's master potters, and his work spread throughout the country — indeed, the world. It was exhibited in the Smithsonian Institute, the Metropolitan Museum of Art, and many other museums.

Simplicity was Ben Owen's guide. He was deeply influenced by the oriental masters. He once wrote that quietness, modesty of form, and harmony were the elements he strived to achieve in a piece of pottery. His work was beautiful and highly prized. It was, in fact, so highly prized that he had trouble keeping up with demand.

"I couldn't keep anything," he says with a chuckle. "They would keep me bought up, cleaned out as fast as I could get it finished."

Despite the demand, he never took advantage. He always kept his prices low. "Everybody fussed at me that come here and bought, said I ought to get more for it. Well, I says, I wanted to keep it so that everybody who would like to have some could get it."

Jacques Busbee died in 1947, and Ben Owen stayed on, working for his widow. He remained until 1959, when Jugtown was sold.

Then he built the kilns out behind the workshop next to his house and began working for himself. The demand for his work remained constant.

"I could've sold a lot more than I did," he says. "There was somebody there wanting something about every day, and on Saturday it was one sight, people coming out from everywhere."

No crowds come anymore. Ben fought hard to keep working. Arthritis had bothered him for years but he continued working, although the pain was often severe. He kept working even as he watched his hands losing control, gradually drawing inward, crippling him. Finally, when he could no longer walk, and his hands could no longer form the clay, against his will, he had to quit.

He had an operation on his knee and it has improved enough for him to get around with the help of the walker. But his crippled hands will never again be able to produce the beautiful forms they once did.

"I haven't been in my shop in over a year," he says, leaning back in his rocking chair. "I miss being out there, meeting the people and seeing the people and . . . you know . . . working. It's taken me quite a while to get adjusted."

October, 1973
Seagrove, North Carolina

Otelia Connor
Keeper of the Manners

"Otelia Connor?" The student grinned. "Well, let's see. She's the kind of lady you expect your grandmother to be, I guess. She seems like a pretty nice little old lady . . ."

I didn't know Otelia Connor, unofficial Keeper of Manners for 15,000 University of North Carolina students, but from what I'd heard about her, I figured she probably would have laughed at the student's description.

I was merely trying to build my nerve to meet her. I had been dredging my mind all day in search of the good manners learned in childhood but lost somewhere along the way. The only thing that kept popping up was: "Don't smack when you eat."

I trudged across the street from Graham Memorial Hall, the campus student union, to the Village Apartments, reminding myself to say "Yes ma'm" and "No ma'm" and not to interrupt when she was talking. It was getting dark. I paused outside the apartment building to straighten my tie, specially donned for this occasion, pushed my hair out of my eyes and disposed of my chewing gum. I braced myself, went inside, climbed the stairs and, at precisely the hour of my appointment, I knocked on the door of Apartment 18.

Otelia Connor came to the door wearing a housecoat and loafers. She had been watching TV, she said. At 74, she is short, with a touch of silver in her hair, and a raspy voice. She smokes incessantly. "But I don't inhale," she hastened to point out. She doesn't look like the sort of person who would clout anybody with an umbrella.

The one-room efficiency apartment is a grandmother's room, without doubt. It contains two antique chairs, a single bed, writing table and lots of fancily framed photographs of children, grandchildren and distinguished ancestors. The wall above the bed is devoted to Otelia Connor, philosopher, as a poster advertising one of her campus talks proclaims. Framed editorial cartoons featuring Otellia hang there with newspaper pictures of her, a *Time* magazine story about her, a poem a student wrote about her.

Otelia Connor came to Chapel Hill in 1957 for her son's graduation from law school. She liked the town and the university cam-

71

pus, and she decided to stay for a while and take some courses.

"The last thing I ever thought I'd be doing was correcting peoples' manners," she told me. "But I soon realized that somebody ought to do it, so I started."

Students soon learned to keep a watch for Otelia.

"Are you a Carolina gentleman?" she might demand. "Well, a gentleman holds a door for a lady."

"Don't you say 'huh' to me!"

Or a student might feel a tap on the shoulder and hear a raspy voice say, "Only common people chew gum in public."

She began writing letters about atrocious manners to the editor of the *Daily Tar Heel*, the campus newspaper, and to other area newspapers. She wrote them by the dozens. In 1963 she hit her peak. Her manners crusade spread across the country and beyond through TV, newspapers and magazines, primarily because of one little incident.

"Well, one day I hit some one on the leg," she was saying. "I went up there at the Tar Heel office. One of the students there, this old writer, had his feet up on the table and he wouldn't take them down so I had my umbrella and I hit him. And he wrote that up."

The intensity of her crusade has slackened lately, but she still prowls the campus every day and fires off an occasional letter to the editor. She isn't sure the crusade will continue when she is no longer able to carry the banner. "It doesn't pay anything," she said. "I don't know who will do it."

The interview was over. I hesitantly asked about my manners. Otelia Connor said I seemed to be a very well-mannered young man. I felt good as I walked back across the street to Graham Memorial Hall, where a felow reporter was busy on another assignment. "She said I did all right," I told him and sank into one of the big, soft chairs to wait for him to finish his work. It was warm in the building and I slipped a little deeper into the chair, propped my feet on the table before me and was soon dozing.

WHACK!!!

I jolted upright. Otelia Connor, wearing a dress of psychedelic pastel colors, stood before me, a roll of newspapers in her hand.

"I didn't think I would find you over here like this," she said, shaking her head.

"Me either," I said, grinning sheepishly.

May, 1968
Chapel Hill, North Carolina

Norman Woodlieff
Carolina Rambler

Gaunt and pale, he sits on the couch in his neat, mill-hill house, and with bony fingers, he pinches the side of his shirt.

"There's no flesh on my bones," he says. "Nothing but ribs there. Went to losing weight, lost my appetite, poor circulation. Loss of that appetite is what done it. Every mouthful I eat at the table I have to force down. It's been two or three years now. I been to the doctor but I can't get straightened out, can't get no strength, get discouraged. If I had a million dollars I'd give every penny just to gain 15 or 20 pounds and have a good appetite again before I leave this earth."

He is 77 now, and not many people would recognize his name, Norman Woodlieff. No doubt few, if any, of the glittering stars of country music today ever heard of him. In the history of country music, Norman Woodlieff is mentioned only in the most obscure and scholarly journals. But he was a country music pioneer, one of the first country musicians ever recorded. In the '20s and '30s, Norman Woodlieff recorded 56 songs for several of the major recording companies. He wrote dozens of songs.

"Hillbilly!" he says, emphatically. "That's what we called it back then."

Norman Woodlieff was 12 when he learned to play the guitar. An older brother helped him learn. "First song I ever learned," he says, beginning to recite, "was, 'Standing on a corner, smokin' a cheap cigar, waitin' on a freight train to catch a empty car. If a brakeman sees me, he'll throw me overboard. Where you goin' fella? I'm goin' on down the road.' I don't remember it all."

At age 13, he went to work in the cotton mill in what was then the town of Spray ("Worked 60-some hours and brought home a payday of five dollars and a half, 13 years old."), where he stayed until he went into the Navy at 19. Two years later, he returned home and met a banjo picker named Charlie Poole. They teamed with Poole's brother-in-law Posey Rorer, called themselves the Carolina Ramblers and began playing at schoolhouse square dances. "We'd take trips up in Virginia," Norman Woodlieff recalls. "We went one time all over West Virginia. Wound up one time in Ironton, Ohio."

In 1925, the year the Grand Ol' Opry was born, the three of

them were working in a railroad car plant in Passaic, New Jersey, and one day Charlie Poole caught a ferry to New York and talked to people at Columbia Records. The next day, the Carolina Ramblers went to New York and recorded four songs, "May I Sleep In Your Barn Tonight, Mister?", "Don't Let Your Deal Go Down Blues," "The Girl I Left In Sunny Tennessee" and "I'm The Man That Rode The Mule Around the World."

The Carolina Ramblers became one of the best known of the early hillbilly groups, but Charlie Poole, the featured singer, reaped most of the fame. When the group went to New York to record again the following year, Norman Woodlieff didn't go with them. "I was expecting all the time to go back with him the second time. Lo and behold, he come by the house one day, had Posey and Roy Harvey in the car with him, said, 'Well, we're goin' to New York.' Was kind of a surprise to me."

Norman Woodlieff continued to play with Charlie Poole, but he did not record again until 1929 when he and Walter Smith and Posey Rorer, who'd had a falling out with his brother-in-law, formed a group and recorded 12 songs for Gennett Records. "They'd give us different names and put 'em out under different labels, but they didn't seem to sell much," he recalls.

In 1931, the year Charlie Poole died at age 39 ("He got to drinkin' too much."), Norman Woodlieff recorded 18 songs for Columbia and Crown with two different groups, the Carolina Buddies and the Virginia Dandies. But the Depression wiped out the record business, and it wasn't until 1939 that he formed a group called Four Pickled Peppers and recorded 10 songs for Bluebird. The group recorded 10 more in 1940. "We had planned to go back again, but we never did," he says. "Something about a union came up. They told us we couldn't make no more records unless we joined that union."

Norman Woodlieff never made any more records. He already had gone into the sign-painting business and that became his life's work. His records and songs never brought him fame or fortune, but he isn't bitter, he says, that he never became a country music star.

"Naw. I tell you, I couldn't've never made it no way. I'd've liked to've done it, but I don't suppose I ever had enough confidence in myself. I just didn't have what it took, to tell the truth about it. I didn't have the determination, know what I mean?"

It has been three or four years since he closed his sign painting shop ("My memory fails me."). He hasn't sung in years. He can't remember when he last played his guitar.

"Can't get him interested in anything," says his wife, Inez. "He don't play his guitar anymore, don't play his tape recorder."

"I've been sort of in a depressed state," he says. "It's boredom, nothing to do, no car. Friends that used to come by to see me don't come by too much anymore. I admit I set around too much. Boredom will tear at you."

He lowers his head and begins to cry, wringing his hands. "Nervous, nervous, nervous. Fear is one of the tormentingest things ever come into a person's life."

He takes up a small Bible and reads a passage from Joshua advising strength and courage. "I believe that. I've tried my best. I've prayed over it. I just don't know what it is that makes a man afraid."

December, 1978
Eden, North Carolina

Lester Singleton
Fort Builder

"Black Ankle Fort," reads the little sign on the big millstone out by the road. It's Lester Singleton's own little joke.

"Used to be," he says, beginning to explain, "they counted this place . . . well, they made so much likker, you know. You can say anything about Black Ankle and, you know, the first thing that pops into anybody's mind is likker. Now they didn't make that likker because they just wanted to make likker. Most of 'em had a wife and children they had to make a living for somehow. You know, you hear people say, 'That old man, he's sorry; he don't do nothing but make likker.' But that ain't no sorry man the way I look at it.

"Making likker's hard work. I've lugged a few barrels through the woods, carried a few hundred pounds of sugar on my back. I'm a son-of-a-gun, if you don't think that there's hard work, you just try it one time. Anyway, Black Ankle always did have a bad name, and I always did tell 'em we ought to have a fort here. But, you know, I wouldn't know where to git a drop of likker now if I was snakebit, not in this community."

It's been a long time since Lester made any liquor, but he did build his fantasy fort, built it with his own hands out of rock and junk.

At this moment he is fretting. "This place ain't nothin' but a mess," he keeps saying, although nothing seems particulary amiss. "See, we had a party here Halloween night. Fifteen hundred people come through this thing. I sure wish you could've come before the flowers all died. Boy, I tell you, I had some nice-uns. See, the frost has got 'em now. The frost has got the most of 'em."

Lester Singleton is a slight, wiry man with a rutted face that makes him look older than his 57 years. He laughs a lot, revealing stained, gapped front teeth. He usually wears work clothes with a grease-smudged railroadman's hat pushed back on his head. He has lived since childhood in Black Ankle, a community straddling the line dividing Randolph and Montgomery Counties, once notorious as a bootlegging center. In addition to making a little liquor, he has done other work.

"I've carpentered," he says. "I raised 10 young'uns, five girls

76

and five boys. They didn't have what they wanted to eat, but they had plenty of it, sich as it was. Last eight year, I've hauled trash. I'm through by about 9:30 or 10:00 in the morning, then I piddle around here the rest of the time."

It was all the piddling that built the fort. He started it back in the '40s; in the beginning it was just to be a stone house for his family. He built four rooms, then added another three onto the back as his family grew. The rest he did just for fun.

He built a big room onto the front of the house, a room he filled with old stuff. It is a public room with a huge stone fireplace in the center, stone benches, tables, big stone planters where greenery grows in profusion under skylights, a stone aquarium where catfish and bream swim. Then he went to work outside, building gardens, a waterfall, covered walkways, a mystery house, fun house, spook house, game booths, and he enclosed it all with a stockade of birch and bamboo.

"I done ever bit of it," he says, standing in the big public room. "I moved this stuff 31 mile in a pickup truck, rock, beams, ever'thing, 31 mile. Ever bit of this come from my daddy's homeplace down below Troy yonder. They call it Loving Hill. I ain't got a thing in the world only what's salvage, just what come out of the junkyard. Ever bit of it's salvage stuff. See that big winder yonder? That ain't nothin' but a door that come out of a store.

"I'd haul a load or two of rock, then I'd haul a load or two of sand, and then I'd come back and put it together. See, I didn't do all this at one time. I done it 15 minutes to two hours at a time. See, I had to live while I was doing it. Them timbers there's over 200 year old, come from where my daddy was raised. See, this is part of a old rock fence. I guess the slaves put up them rock when it was first put up, you know what I mean? Now this is creek rock."

He moves quickly around the room, feeling the timbers and rocks as he talks. "This is the original chimney. This here thing's 200 year old."

Lester loves to talk and tell stories and there is almost always somebody around to listen. Many of his children and grand-children live on or around his 12 acres of rocky ground, and many other relatives live close by and drop in frequently. Everybody is welcome at Lester's fort. People from throughout the community gather in the big front room almost every night and especially on weekends.

"On weekends," he says, "it's a sight to see. Young people

mostly. Young'uns, they really come around here. I declare if they don't . . . No, hunh-huh, don't charge 'em a dime. I've never charged nobody nothin'. See, what made me do this was just for the community. Just to have a recreation place for the community. This is a poor community. We never did have nothin' in here that would help the community."

It was mostly for the young people that he installed the $750 stereo outfit and tape player in the big front room. "Lord, we have fun with that thing. We get in here and just have a big time. I git a kick out of it. I really do."

The cookouts are for the entire community. They're held twice a month at the fort. Almost always a hundred or more people show up. They eat, have treasure hunts, play ball-toss and bottle games at booths out back, giggle through the spook house and mystery house. Lester keeps the place lighted like a carnival. The only charge is for the meal, and it isn't much. The money goes into a special fund.

"It goes to help the community. If anybody gits burned out or anything. We keep two months supply of groceries on hand for a family of six in case anybody gits down and needs it. It's just a little something to help 'em along. 'Nother words, to keep 'em off the welfare, you know what I mean?"

Strangers are also welcome at Lester's fort, and he likes nothing better than taking them on tours of the place. "Now, how come me to cover this walk?" he asks, leading the way outside. "You don't have any idy, I guess . . ." and he is launched into an explanation of how old houses had kitchens out back, separate from the house, and how people needed to keep out of the weather while going from one to the other, and how that gave him the idea. Then he is bouncing down the walk saying, "There's what we call the gov'ment tree." It's a willow of some type, about 20 feet tall. He rooted it in a soft drink bottle four years earlier and it grew dramatically.

"Now, how come me to call this the gov'ment tree?" He grins. "See, they ain't a straight place on that tree, even the leaves are crooked." He cackles. "And it looks like it's about to die all the time."

The container vegetable garden is next. "See, here's how I raise my stuff, raise it in buckets." He also uses barrels, soft drink boxes, freezers, washing machine tubs, anything that will hold organic matter, all gathered from trash piles. "Git a world of stuff out of these things. I raise all I need right out of these containers. I had one punkin vine in that tub yonder, got 27 punkins off that thing."

Recorded screams erupt from the spook house when Lester flips a switch, and electrified skulls and other scary things glow in the dark. "I done that this year," he says. "See, at Halloween we had a fortune teller and everything."

Two big hollowed-log feed troughs stand like monuments out by the road and Lester pauses by them. "Them things is 200 year old. They come from the old homeplace. They was just handed down from generation to generation. You know, they got one of them down there at the Indian mound, call it a canoe. Ain't nothin' but a feed trough. I didn't say nothin' to 'em about it but . . . you know, a Indian'd have more sense than to git in that. He'd drown."

Now Lester is scurrying about showing off his millstones, his own watergate ("I had that sign up before anybody ever heard of that Watergate mess."), his waterfall and waterwheel, which he sets to gurgling with a flick of a switch ("That's just a old basement pump in there and that tank's just a old deep freeze from the junkyard, holds about 18 hundred gallon of water."), his mystery hill house ("This is our crazy house. See, young'uns love to see this ball roll uphill."), the bottle museum with all its carefully arranged gags and old things ("Just pick them up here, there and yonder, trash piles mostly. Yeah, most of 'em, we scratched 'em out of trash piles.").

Coming out of the bottle museum, Lester stops to look out across a field where he has dug a small pond. Piles of dirt are scattered over the field. "I'm goina fix that up for the little young'uns," he says. "Put some swings and this and that and t'other out there for the *little* young'uns. They goina play summers, you know what I mean, and I'd just as soon they'd play here as anywhere."

In his flower garden, he sits to rest on a wall made of old railroad ties. "You know," he says, "I come up in the great tribulations. We made our own fun. We sawed our wheels out of blackgum trees to make our wagons. We had to make our own fun. You know, people my age, a lot of 'em, they jealous of the way these young people coming up now. That's what I think."

After all these years, Lester is still making his own fun. And sharing it freely. And he has no plans to stop.

" 'Nother words, we're going to be doin' somethin' as long as we live, you know it? And I'd just as soon be doin' somethin' like this as anything. Don't make no money, but we do have a good time, you know. I love to fool around here, you know it? I get a

79

Just Folks
big kick out of it."

November, 1975
Black Ankle, North Carolina

Aunt Georgia McTier
Visions of Beauty

Sister had a bad night, and so in the afternoon Aunt Georgia lay down beside her to catch a little nap. But she is up quickly at the knock, feeling her way by the rope strung over the bed.

She laughs about the rope. "You see we've got ropes up. You'd think we're taking in laundry, but that's the way we have to go."

Aunt Georgia has been blind for 25 years, a victim of glaucoma. She sits in a chair at the foot of the bed where her sister Addie lies motionless. She is s small woman, Aunt Georgia, with steel gray hair topped by a black hairnet. Her white sweater is buttoned at the throat. She laughs easily.

"There were 12 of us," she says. "Only two left now."

I ask about her age. "I give it as 93," she says with a laugh, "but I think it's 97. I'll leave it 93. Quite a young girl. My sister's 90. She taught school for 50 years, been sick 14 years now. She teaches right on, but there's nobody to listen."

Aunt Georgia McTier's given name is Georgianna but she doesn't like it very much. "I always thought mules had names like that," she says. She was born on a farm in Browns Summit. Her father raised tobacco and wanted his children to be educated. He'd sweep the dirt in the backyard, give all the children sticks and make them work math problems. "He'd walk around the yard and whistle and sing while we did multiplication," Aunt Georgia recalls. "He'd sit us down at night and give us spelling."

When the children grew old enough to go to college, the family moved to Greensboro and bought a two-story house beside Emmanuel Lutheran College. Her father wanted his children to have opportunities that few other black children got. Five of them went on to finish college, and Sister Addie got a master's degree; but Georgianna was not among their number. She had to quit and go to work. "Somebody had to help pay the bills," she says.

The college is gone now, as are all but one of her brothers and sisters; but the big house is still standing, and so is Aunt Georgia, now tending to her ailing sister. While Sister Addie was teaching all those years in the Lutheran School, Aunt Georgia was teaching too. She worked 50 years for a prominent family, rearing three generations of children, "my white children," she calls them, and they are scattered now from New Orleans to California. Now and then, one of them will send a ticket, and Aunt Georgia, who never married, will get on an airplane, and wearing a big tag on her coat that says "Totally Blind," she will fly off to visit one of her "children," carrying along some of her work, because if there is one thing Aunt Georgia believes in, it is keeping busy.

Tending to her sister helps keep her busy now. Her sister suffered a stroke in 1958. She was recovering from that, although she too was going blind from glaucoma, when one day her housecoat caught fire while she was frying apples. She ran screaming through the house to Georgia who put the fire out with her hands and ripped the garment from her. Sister Addie had third degree burns. Aunt Georgia also suffered severe burns. Since that time, Sister Addie has spent most of her time in bed, closely attended by Aunt Georgia and by Maggie, a woman who lives with them.

"Sister was so bad last night," Aunt Georgia says. "We were giving her peaches and whole wheat bread at 3 o'clock last night. I take care of her just like a baby. We have to feed her. She can't feed herself. But she eats well. She eats very well. She's got so she sleeps in the daytime and at night she wants to get up and walk around the house and go to class. Oh, she was a smart sister. She's a smart one all right. She was always leading everything. They said she was the smartest thing. She just had brains. I tell her she got some of mine." She laughs. "She can speak German, speak it so good. People used to come just to hear her speak German. I wish she'd speak some now so you could hear her, but she hasn't been talking much lately."

There are dolls in the room, and sometimes Sister Addie will cry for them, as she did when she was a little girl, and Aunt Georgia is always there to get them for her, to soothe her. "I take care of her just like a baby," she repeats.

You don't have to be around Aunt Georgia long to realize she is a remarkable woman. She is spritely and hard-working and her wit is keen, as is her appreciation of beauty, although she cannot see. Flowers adorn the room, roses and dahlias she grew. She preserves her flowers in wax, dries and frames them, as she does stalks of wheat and fall leaves. She does not have to be able to see them to know how beautiful they are. "I can't even keep one if I fix one," she says. "Somebody will come here and want it."

Music used to fill the house. Aunt Georgia still sings now and then, old songs and hymns. "Sister sold the piano," she says. "All I have now is a steel guitar and it needs strings." She laughs again. "It's aged too. Then I blow a harp with a piece of tissue

82

paper. And sing? And how!"

She also washes, irons and sews, using what she calls "blind needles." She gets one to show how easily she can thread it. "There. Isn't that wonderful? That shows we shouldn't get despondent. When we lose something, we always get something back." She makes quilts, too, and Maggie fetches a beautiful one made from horse show ribbons. "That's how I make a little extra change," says Aunt Georgia. "That's what I do most all the time, day and night. That's the way I buy my oil."

Her face beams. "I don't let myself get helpless. No, you mustn't stop. That's what I keep telling Sister. No, we mustn't feel sorry for ourselves. We should be thankful. We have a shelter over us, pretty good food . . . I think we got a lot to be thankful for. If Sister was well, of course, it would be better."

I ask if she is satisfied with the way her life has gone. "Beautiful!" she says and laughs a full, hearty laugh. "Listen, I can't do a thing about it . . . might as well be."

September, 1970
Greensboro, North Carolina

83

Odell Mayo
Broom Shuffler

Don't call it sweeping. Odell Mayo is quick to correct anybody about that.

"Shufflin' the broom," he says. "What you call shufflin' the broom. It's not sweepin'. Lotta people call it sweepin' but it's not sweepin'. No sir. If you had to sweep, you wouldn't never get too much done. Hunh-unh. Wouldn't get nowhere. Shufflin' the broom, spinnin' the broom. It's kinda hard to spin that broom if you don't know your business."

He gives a little demonstration, one broom in each hand, both moving briskly up the sidewalk in perfect synchronization. "Now that's what you call shufflin' the broom."

When it comes to shufflin' the broom, Odell Mayo is a virtuoso. He is a familiar sight on the streets of Hillsborough as he makes his way, both brooms flying, his voice booming greetings and songs. His job is to keep the streets clean and the grass cut in the town's two cemeteries, but a stranger might think him the town's official greeter as well.

"Best broom you can use," he is saying, "is these nylon brooms. Stuff like these ain't no count. I'm going to get me some big brooms here next week, good brooms. Yes sir . . . Hey, Mr. Hunt, how you doin'?"

The man passing on the sidewalk greets him and says, "You doing a good job."

Yes, sir, but it's a lot to be done yet."

The man passes on up the street and Odell Mayo says, "I been working for this town ever since the first mayor was elected. Ben Johnson. Mayor Ben Johnson. That was some years back. They didn't have too many men then. Yes sir. Cleanin' these streets, taking care of these streets. Trying to make the old place look like something. 'Course, it's purty hard on the old boy, but I does the best I can."

All those years of shuffling brooms around the streets have given Odell Mayo an uncommon strength. He sometimes mows with two push mowers at the same time, one in each hand. "Yeah, I'm a little skinny but I'm a purty strong man," he says, holding out his hands. "I got 879 pounds of pressure in each hand. Yes sir. That's a lot of pressure, ain't it? It come from hard work. Hard work and exercise.

"I had a Caterpillar tractor run over me. Been hit by three cars. Ain't dead yet. Still living. Still living. Yes sir. Thought one time I'd never walk again. I got out and walked all over the country, walked to Greensboro, back over here toward Raleigh, up around Virginia. I walk from here to Durham in about an hour and a half. It takes a good man to keep up with these brooms. Yes sir."

He stops his brooms to ponder a question. "How long can I keep it up? I keep it up from day to day. That's how long I keep it up."

"You can keep it up all day, can't you?" says a merchant from the doorway of a nearby store.

"Yes sir, I can keep it up all day. Yes sir. I sure can."

Odell Mayo is 49. He lives with a brother now that his mother is dead. He never married. "I just ain't ready for no marriage. No sir. A good woman's hard to find, you know? Naw, I could've been married two or three times. I got engaged one time. She was a Cherokee Indian. I let her go. I was more devoted to my Mama. My Mama meant the whole world to me. More than anybody in the world except the Lord. He comes first, you know. Mama's been gone about nine, almost 10 months. Just six of us living now. My Mama had all boys. No girls at all. Just eight strapping young men."

Odell Mayo knows almost everybody in Hillsborough and he greets most of the residents by name as he passes. "I been living here almost 30 years, and I don't have no trouble with nobody. I don't go ahead and bother nobody and I tends to my business. I know different hexes you can put on people and they can't break it, but I don't bother nobody. I always try to greet everybody with a smile and treat everybody with respect. And I tends to my business."

Suddenly, he spots several people sitting in a car parked across the street and he waves and calls, "Hey, sugar, I see y'all over there. How you doin'? Who's that? Is that Grandma in there?" He is at the car window now. "Hey, honey. How you doin'? Y'all mighty good people. Take care of yourself . . ." And he is off again, shuffling his brooms on down the street.

September, 1976
Hillsborough, North Carolina

Mickey Walsh
'Orse Trainer

You expect, perhaps, a squire, genteelly overseeing his manor. So it is a bit of a surprise to find him sweeping out the stables. His long-sleeve shirt is buttoned at the collar and sleeves. The snap of his khaki work pants droops below his belt. Over his white hair, pulled down on his forehead, he wears a flat cap, the kind golfers and rakes used to wear.

His pug nose, crooked smile and lively eyes would betray him even if his heavy brogue did not. He is thoroughly Irish. He grins when you apologize for knowing nothing about horses.

"There's nobody knows anything about 'orses," he says, "and the older I get the more I believe it. There's nothing can make a liar out of you like a 'orse. Every day. That they can do."

If anybody knows anything about horses, Mickey Walsh does. For 40 years, he has been one of the country's top trainers of thoroughbred horses. Horses he has trained and owned have won hundreds of thousands of dollars. Not only does he train and own horses (45 at present), he also owns a racetrack. He built his mile-long track in the late 1940s on the edge of Southern Pines and here he founded the Stoneybrook Steeplechase, an event attended by thousands of people each year. No little accomplishment for an immigrant who arrived in this country at age 19 with little more than a love for horses.

He grew up in Kildorrey, County Cork, Ireland, where his father was a pub owner and horse trader. Horses were a part of his life for as far back as he can remember. He was riding at age eight, racing as a teen-ager. At 19, seeing no future in Ireland, he set sail for New York, hoping to find opportunity. "I had no idea of getting mixed up with 'orses when I came here," he says.

He was wandering wide-eyed through New York when he walked down to Columbus Circle and saw some horses in a park. He started talking to the owners and found his first job — as stable boy at a New Jersey farm. He didn't work long before he became seriously ill, unable to work. He lost the job, but after his recovery, found another working with polo ponies and hunting horses on Long Island. A job with a riding school in Great Neck followed. He was running his own riding school when he was talked into going to work training show horses for W.L. Kennedy,

87

a wealthy Boston owner of clothing stores.

The Kennedy family owned a horse farm near Southern Pines and that brought Mickey Walsh to North Carolina. He liked the area, and three years after his first visit to the state, he bought a 36-acre farm called Stoneybrook near Southern Pines. Soon he began buying adjoining land. "And stupidly built a racetrack," he says, smiling with obvious pride.

He started the Stoneybrook Steeplechase in 1948 ("The jumping racket I've liked all my life"), and it has grown every year. For some, the races are a grand social event. Picnics are spread behind Rolls Royces, complete with candelabra, crystal, silver, fine china, iced champagne and butlers in tails. Many of the spectators dress as if they were attending a formal dinner with the President.

"Just put on the dog," says Frank Brawley, a friend of Mickey's, who helps stage the races. "But today the majority of the people who come are just average people who come here for a nice day."

For Mickey and his wife, Kitty, the races are mostly work, but they also are occasion for an annual reunion of their far-scattered seven children and 27 grandchildren. Kitty is a jovial woman who likes to tease her husband. They were schoolmates in Ireland. She came to this country two years after he did but denies she came to marry him. "I just came over and that was it. We decided to hook up together." The hook-up has lasted 51 years. Kitty loves to cook and on race day she prepares a lavish spread for her family — plus 400 guests.

On this day, she bustles in the kitchen of the Walsh's modest brick house on the edge of the racetrack, preparing a big, hot lunch for her husband, Frank Brawley and son-in-law Grady McCollum, the Stoneybrook Farm manager.

The talk is of horses and racing. "Is there anything else?" asks Kitty. A few days earlier, a horse she owns, Crag's Corner, won the Carolina Cup in the steeplechase at Camden, South Carolina. "We talk about horses mornin', noon and night," she says, "and if you bring up any other subject, nobody's interested."

Independence. Rhythminhim, King Commander. Erin's Son. The proud names tick off. All winners. All trained and owned by Mickey Walsh. Just a few of his many winners.

And Little Squire. Nobody who saw him can forget Little Squire. "He was the one and only," Mickey says. "I guess he's been the talk of the world over the years. He was unbelievable, that fellow." A show horse. World champion open jumper at Madison Square Garden, 1939, Mickey Walsh astride. They were in Movietone News.

"Yeah, he was a good pony," Mickey says, smiling. "I was his only handicap."

Little Squire was a small white horse. He could jump more than seven feet high. Like Mickey, he came from Ireland. He was brought to Mickey out of desperation by his owner because nobody else could handle him.

"With his Irish brogue, the horse just loved him," Kitty says. "He really did, didn't he, Michael?"

"He never told me," Mickey says with a grin.

From May until November, Mickey and Kitty stay on the road with their horses, following the steeplechase circuit. The rest of the year, they work at the farm. "Lots of labor," says Mickey. "That's what 'orses are. Nothin' but work, work and more work. I guess you have to have a love for them. That's all there is to it. If I didn't have a horse tomorrow, I'd just as soon not be around."

He is up by five each morning, feeding horses by 5:30. Three grandsons, Michael III, Kevin and Dan, come each morning to gallop horses for two hours before school (Michael, a high school senior in his third year of riding the farm's horses on the steeplechase circuit, rides six hours every day). Then the stables must be cleaned, horses must be let in and out of pasture, repairs must be made, horses must be worked in the training corral. It all makes for a long day.

"Got no kicks," says Mickey, pausing in the stable. "I've had a good life, thanks-be-Lord. I've been a very lucky person. I'm like the old 'orse now. He don't talk back. He does the best he can."

April, 1978
Southern Pines, North Carolina

Fred and Nellie McIntyre
Creative Piddlers

"You know the difference between a professional and an amateur?" Fred McIntyre asked me. "The professional covers up his mistakes and the amateur don't know how."

Fred and his wife, Nellie, were showing me around their place. We were talking about their snug house. It was the house Fred was born in 64 years earlier. While Fred was still in diapers, his father died, leaving Fred's mother with five children, a drafty three-room house with a mud-daubed chimney and 15 scrubby hilltop acres on which to eke out a living. Somehow they managed.

After Fred and Nellie married, Fred decided he wanted to buy the old family place and did, paying $16 an acre, a fair price at the time. The house was run-down, the soil so exhausted some of it wouldn't even grow weeds. But through the years, with lots of hard work and vision but very little money, Fred and Nellie managed to turn the place into a garden spot, so lush and lovely that people come from miles around just to see it.

Fred fixed up the house himself, remodeling, adding onto it from time to time, paneling the walls with pine he cut on the place. He knew nothing about carpentry or the building trades when he started and claims he still doesn't know much. "You don't have to know nothing on an old house," he said. "Just get up there and start. Anything you do to it's goina help it. I'm not a mason, but I built that chimney right there. A mason might find fault with it, but it works."

For more than 25 years, while Fred and Nellie's five children were growing up, Fred worked as an upholsterer in a furniture plant. "I liked it, but I got tired of it," he says. "It got boresome." He quit 13 years ago and went to work at a rug plant where he stayed seven years. He quit that too. There just were too many other things he wanted to do, things he usually calls 'piddlin'.

"Let me see if I can get my toys runnin'," Fred said. His toys are a miniature village he built out under the trees on the edge of one of Nellie's flower gardens. The village is powered by water-wheels and that includes the people in it, mechanical figures Fred carved from wood. A woman washes clothes in a tub, loggers saw a tree, a man chops wood, logs pass through a sawmill, a horsedrawn wagon circles the village, the church bell rings, a music box plays. "Me and the neighborhood boys built this," Fred explained. "They come up with the idy and I come up with the reality. See, I got two little grandboys. They're four years old. They're *some* characters. They were here to see me this weekend. They don't tear things up; they just kinda get 'em out of workin' order. Oh, they're characters. I tell you they are. They got everything wrecked but I wouldn't take a million dollars for 'em. Them two little boys, they have theirselves a ball around here."

A lot of people come to the McIntyre's place just to see Fred's village. One Sunday when he was away, he left a guestbook by the village with a little note asking people to sign it. When he returned home that night, the book contained 150 signatures.

Some people also come to see Fred's fish. They are fat bream that live in a little pond Fred built so he'd have a place to teach his children to swim. We walked toward the edge of the pond. Fred was carrying three slices of bread. "Now you watch," he said, "they'll gather in. They don't run from you, they run to you. They'll follow us right along. They'll all be there when I get there. They know where I feed 'em."

Sure enough, the fish began tagging along beside him, and others started coming from all directions, like chicken rushing toward a bucket of scratch feed. At a certain spot, Fred knelt by the water and the fish came up and began to eat from his hand. Some of the fish will even cradle in Fred's palm and let him lift them from the water. "They're not the least bit bashful," Fred said. "You don't scare these fish."

Many people come, too, to see Nellie's flowers. Every year, she plants large beds of many varieties, carefully arranged. She grows hundreds of house plants and thousands of bedding plants for her big organic garden. Until recently, she had a job at a mill, but working eight hours a day left her little time for tending her flowers and plants. "I decided one had to go and I couldn't lose the flowers," she said, "so I quit."

"She wouldn't let me work in the flowers," Fred said, smiling. "She'll let me fix up the bed, and after that it's 'Get out, get out,' and I don't create any argument at all."

That leaves Fred time for his "piddlin." In a small cluttered shop next to the house, he makes furniture for his children and friends. He built all of his own furniture, most of it from solid walnut. He also built a greenhouse for Nellie on the south side of the house. "That thing is worth its weight in gold," Fred says. On sunny winter days, by opening certain windows in the house to create a draft, the greenhouse heats the whole house. Fred also built a contraption of large black plastic pipe in the top of the greenhouse and that provides most of their hot water.

"They ain't nothin' to it," he said. "They's nothin' complicated about it, and it didn't cost much. I tell you one thing, it's payin' off. That cut our power bill $15 a month."

Now Fred is in the process of building Nellie a bigger greenhouse. He's doing all the work himself, of course.

We stood out in the orchard, under trees hanging heavy with fruit, and Fred and Nellie talked about how lucky they were and I couldn't help but think of what a perfect example they are of how luck is so often built on hard work and heart work. "I'm enjoyin' life the most I ever have in my life," Fred was saying. "Just to tell you the truth about it, I am."

August, 1978
Troy, North Carolina

Russell Powell
Hiz Honor the Symphony Conductor

"You're standing in it," Russell Powell said. "Pinedene Mayor's Office, Pinedene Symphony Hall, Pinedene Community College, Pinedene Medical Center, Pinedene Rescue Squad . . ."

"Have we got a rescue squad?" asked one of the boys, looking up from his guitar.

Russell Powell nodded. "That wheelbarrow out back."

There are heretics who try to claim that Pinedene does not exist, that it just a small section of Southern Pines. People in Pinedene do not see it that way. They will tell you that Southern Pines and the closeby towns of Pinehurst and Aberdeen are mere suburbs of Pinedene.

The center of community life in Pinedene is one end of a small cement-block building on Old Highway 1 at the southern edge of Southern Pines. Signs outside identify it as the Pinedene Jazz Center. Pay no attention to those. It is far more than that.

Here presides Russell Powell, self-appointed mayor of Pinedene, conductor of the Pinedene Philharmonic Symphony Orchestra, keeper of the Pinedene lighthouse, dispenser of philosophy and guitar strings. He also plays the mandolin, but that shouldn't be held against him. Here, too, gathers the town council — whenever the members are sober enough — to conduct the town business. At one meeting they voted to open a cat house in Pinedene — for homeless cats, of course.

"We just completed our annual election for S.O.B. of the year," the mayor said.

"Sweet Old Boy," added one of the boys.

"We counted the ballots Valentine's Day," the mayor went on. "Chief of police won. We made up a little plaque and I sent it to him. He hasn't called me to thank me for it or anything." The mayor is convinced there was tampering with the ballot box, though, because he came in sixth.

Sometimes the question is asked, which came first Pinedene or Russell Powell? Russell Powell did, of course. He will tell you that he is "50 damn 9" years old, nearly 10 years older than Pinedene, which began as a housing development that went under in the Crash of '29. By that time, Russell Powell was already preparing himself to fall into bad habits. He took up the guitar as a teen-ager

93

and discovered the mandolin a year later. Women, bourbon and books quickly followed, and after that, there wasn't much hope for Russell Powell.

His father, meanwhile, had opened a service station in Pinedene, and after Russell graduated from high school he went to work there. He stayed in the service station business for 30 years, although during that time the service station evolved into a grocery store, and the store evolved into the Pinedene Jazz Center. The way that happened was that Russell's buddy, Jack Stancil, a mechanic, used to bring his guitar by the service station, and the two of them would sit and pick a few tunes together. Others started coming to listen and still others came to play. One day a local politician dropped in while a jam session was in progress and exclaimed, "I'll be damned, the Pinedene Jazz Center." The name stuck.

With all those musicians coming in, Russell started selling a few guitar strings, because there wasn't any other place to get them nearby. Then he added a few instruments and other incidentals, and it wasn't long before the fiddles and guitars and banjos and mandolins outnumbered the groceries. Ten years ago, the Pinedene Stock Exchange announced a major stock split at the Pinedene Jazz Center. Russell Powell took the stock of instruments and music supplies next door, and another fellow took over the stock of groceries and motor oil. That proved to be a good move for Russell Powell. The grocery store is now a real estate office, but the Pinedene Jazz Center rolls on, an institution.

It is a small and incredibly cluttered place with fiddles, guitars, banjos hanging everywhere, the walls plastered with humorous signs. Five days a week, from noon to five, Russell Powell is apt to be found sitting amidst the clutter by the front window, his mandolin in his lap, or close at hand.

"I'm on duty all the time," he said. "Here we play when we feel like it and if somebody wants to buy something, we take time out for a commercial and sell 'em something."

There is almost always somebody who has come to play or listen, to get into deep discussions or shallow ones, to hear Russell Powell discourse on whatever is on his mind. Anybody is welcome except for proselytizing preachers and Republican office seekers. Even those are occasionally tolerated.

"We have one token Republican," Russell said. "He plays the bass. He's even on the town council here in Southern Pines. We supported him for town council but if he aims any higher, no dice."

The music is apt to range from bluegrass to classical (Russell's own tastes run to classical and jazz), and topics of discussion may range from black holes in space (astronomy is one of Russell's favorite subjects) to the black holes in politics and religion (two more of his favorite subjects). "With the right people, we'll discuss any subject. I went out to the community college not long ago and gave a lecture on atheism to a religion class," Russell said. He told them he didn't know much about the subject. "You don't really know much about atheism. You just find out all about religion, then you become an atheist."

Talk like that, along with all his bad habits, has made Russell Powell a prime target for preachers down through the years. Some have even brought in high-powered reinforcements from great distances to work on him, all to no avail. They had about given up until last year when he fell seriously ill and had to be hospitalized. "Just give me a beer," he protested on the way to the hospital, "I'll be all right." The preachers came then in flocks. "They thought I might be getting ready to sign on for the last trip," he said with a slight smile. They left as usual, shaking their heads and praying.

Russell's illness limited his bad habits somewhat, but not much. Things haven't changed at the Pinedene Jazz Center, and neither are they likely to while he's still around. The Pinedene Symphony Orchestra will still play every Saturday, and it will go on tour several times a year as usual, performing at Moore Memorial Hospital on Christmas, Camp Easter for handicapped children in the summer. The town council will still gather when its members are able, and Russell Powell will continue to preside over town business. Like many public officials, he points to some of his accomplishments with pride. One of these is the Pinedene lighthouse. He built it and put it in the front window of the store to flash every second at the darkness. "We were concerned because several of our mariners were getting into their cups a little," he explained. "Since we put that light up, we haven't had a single shipwreck in Pinedene. One of our harmonica players did get a little off course here one night, though."

And although the responsibilities of keeping Pinedene on course often weigh heavily on him, Russell Powell said, he has no intention of giving up his public duties, despite all the frequent public clamor for his resignation. "To hell with 'em," he said.

March, 1978
Pinedene, North Carolina

95

Hoyle Phillips
Wind-Broke

He likes it best when the wind blows. Then they all turn in unison, clatter-whirling softly, a few of them creaking a little. He sometimes sits in the open door of the small green trailer watching them for hours, entranced. Perhaps it is because his own breath comes so hard now. There are times when he thinks it won't come at all. Emphysema, the doctors have told him. He doesn't understand such fancy words.

"I used to hear my mama and daddy talking about wind-broke horses," he says, "When they're wind-broke, they ain't no good no more. I think that's what I'm like. I just worked too hard for too long."

He worked sawmills mainly, moving with them, sometimes as far away as Mt. Airy, Salisbury, Denton. He was a big man and he was proud he could do the work of two. Occasionally, there were other jobs, but he never had the chance for a good one, an easy one. He never learned to read and write, except to sign his name, Hoyle Phillips.

It wasn't until after his body had betrayed him that he realized how important it was that none of his employers had withheld or paid any Social Security taxes for him. So at 54, wind-broke, unable to work and without income, he sits in the open door of the small trailer and watches the windmills turn.

There are dozens and dozens of them in many shapes and sizes, mounted on poles and towers and other structures amid the clutter and high weeds that surround the trailer. Most are painted in bright colors. "They're purty, ain't they?" he says. "They really fascinate me at times."

He doesn't know why he became so fascinated with windmills. It was just something inexplicable that was always there. "I been makin' 'em off and on ever since I was able to whittle, as far as that's concerned," he says. But it wasn't until he found himself unable to work that he started making them in great numbers. At first he thought he might be able to sell them to bring in a little money and he put them up around the trailer so that people passing on U.S. 64 could see them. But the demand for ornamental windmills, he discovered, was almost non-existent. "Don't sell enough to say I sell any. I 'spect I ain't sold no more than six or seven in the last three year."

Still he continued to make them and put them up around the trailer owned by his son-in-law, where he lives with his wife, Bertha, who suffers from asthma. "I just wanted something nobody else didn't have," he explains. "Something different."

What he really wanted was to build a windmill big enough to live in. Years before, his wife had bought small piece of land near High Rock Lake, and there several years ago, he set to work building what he called his "Holland house." He scrounged materials wherever he could, worked as his breath would allow him, usually only a couple of hours a day. For more than three years he worked on it, until his strength wouldn't allow it anymore. He put 12-foot blades on the front. "I had aimed to put a big shaft on it, put a generator on it and pull my own power," he says, "but it run into too much money."

His "Holland house" still isn't finished, although one of his daughters and her children are temporarily living in it. He doesn't know now if he ever will be able to complete it or live in it. "I hope to before I die. But I don't know. Get weak. Can't hardly get my breath. Gets rough sometimes. I guess you just live as long as you can, die when you can't help it, I don't know."

For now he contents himself building smaller windmills and putting them up with the others to watch them turn. "Build 'em out of scraps. Just picked it up first one place and then another, junkpiles, when I was able. I'm about to run out of material. Don't know what I'll do when my material runs out. I reckon I'll just have to quit makin' 'em, cause I can't afford to buy any."

A breeze has come up. The windmills are busy. He aims a spurt of tobacco juice into the high weeds as he watches them turning. "Just watch these I got, I reckon. I like to watch 'em turn."

September, 1978
Lexington, North Carolina

Pigmeat Markham
Here Come de Judge

"Ohyez. Ohyez. Ohyez. De cou't is now in session. Here come de judge. Here come de judge. O'der in de cou'troom. Here come de judge."

The refrain is just dying in the burst of applause. Pigmeat Markham climbs off the stage and lopes to his dressing room. A sign adorns the door, penned on notebook paper: "Pigmeat & Girls."

He is a big man, 240 pounds, and most of that in the middle. His lips are like two rolls of baloney. He wears baggy pants with suspenders, a little crushed, gray hat on the back of his head, a pin-stripe double-breasted coat that droops almost to his knees. His shoes are on the wrong feet. It is doubtful anybody in the packed audience noticed that. Pigmeat has been wearing his shoes on the wrong feet in his act since he started doing comedy 50 years ago. He sees no reason to change now.

He pushes through the door, strips to his t-shirt and shorts and flops into a rickety yellow chair. He is sweating. Big drops roll off his forehead, over his nose. His chin drips.

"Just like a racehorse," he says. "You don't know you're going until you get to sweating. Then you know you're movin' . . ."

Come September, Pigmeat Markham will have been in show business 51 years. All that time he's been doing the same thing: black situation comedy. He's the only one left doing it now. He's the black Red Skelton. "I set my style and stayed with it," he says.

That style had its beginnings in Durham, where he was born Dewey Markham. His father had been a farmer but moved to town and took a job stoking furnaces. He died when Dewey was three. Dewey, his mother and four sisters were left to fend for themselves.

"I didn't go no farther than third grade," he says. But during those three years he got his introduction to show business. His class put on a play called "20 Minutes in Hell." "They picked me to do the comedy," he recalls.

He was 14 when he left home and joined a carnival with a group of friends, musicians. Dewey became their comic. "They just got you together and put the work on you," he recalls. "Dollar fifty a week and pay your own room and board. Fifty cent a week for a room and they gave you breakfast."

He stayed with the carnival a year before moving on to tent shows, medicine shows. "In those days I was learning and picking up stuff." His idols were a pair of black comedians from Philadelphia, Bilo and Ashes. It was eight years before he played a theater. That happened in Macon, Georgia, and it was there he picked up the name Pigmeat. It came from a bit in which the straight man tried to guess his name. Pigmeat's line went, "My name is Sweet Papa Pigmeat. I got the River Jordan in my lips and all de women is around to be baptized."

He wrote the Here-Come-De-Judge bit in 1928, and he has been doing it regularly since. It took 40 years for it to catch on big. Meanwhile, Pigmeat made it to Broadway in 1929 in a show called "Hot Rhythm." He went on to play the big theaters, the Apollo, the Paramount, always writing his own material, always performing with a straight man and an attractive young woman.

In 1945 he was Alamo the cook on the Andrews Sisters radio show. Two years later he did the judge bit on TV for the first time. "I broke the ice for situation comedy on TV," he says. For a long time he would look back on it as the peak of his career.

In recent years he played one-nighters and small clubs. He made a few comedy albums, but they never sold very well. Then last year, unbeknownst to Pigmeat, Sammy Davis Jr. broke into a chant on the TV show "Laugh-In."

"Here come de judge. Here come de judge . . ."

Within days there were Here-Come-De-Judge bumper stickers, t-shirts, records. Pigmeat was almost left out of his own bit. He huddled with his managers and record company executives. Overnight, he wrote a song, then recorded it.

"It's a very big record, all over the country, boy," he says. "Sold way over a million."

TV shows began seeking him out. Rowan and Martin. Johnny Carson. For the first time, his old albums became hard to find. Now he is on a tour of 50 cities, playing to audiences of thousands.

"I've always been known to colored people," he says. "This is making the white people know me. Now they all want to see who I am."

De judge, it appears, has done arrived . . .

August, 1968
Durham, North Carolina

R.J. Stansbury
Candidate for Governor

The little store was built of concrete blocks and painted red once, long ago. It perches on a dusty hillside in a run-down neighborhood on West King Street. A green kerosene tank with a hand-pump stands by the door, where the Chesterfield salesman hung a thermometer that ceased functioning years ago. A driveway circles the building; at the back, where customers used to park, junk is piled against the wall. The back door sports a Smokey Bear bumper sticker and a sign stenciled in black: "Stansbury For Governor."

R.J. Stansbury was a candidate for governor in the Democrat primary of 1964, one of six candidates. He traveled the state playing a banjo, singing, proclaiming himself the candidate of "the common man." He got 2,145 votes, good enough for last place.

The store is dark and dirty inside. The floor rolls like an uneasy sea. The worn linoleum is awash with dirt, food wrappers, cigarette butts, burned matches. Ceiling and shelves sag. Only dusty canned foods, a few loaves of bread on a rusty rack, three or four half-filled candy boxes in a glass-enclosed counter beckon customers.

A big man sits alone in a corner on an old car seat propped on soft drink crates. He wears an old hat, glasses, an open jacket. A stained white shirt strains to contain his drooping belly. A banjo is parked beside him; a guitar rests on a shelf above his head. He spits tobacco juice into a paint-speckled bucket beside him and wipes his mouth with his sleeve.

"Mr. Stansbury?"

"What's left of me."

It is another election year, and I tell him I have been wondering if he is planning to run again.

"Not unless something gets after me," he says, "I been crippled for three years, Cap'n. I went up here and tried to help 'em set up this mill here, cotton mill, and I set on a cement floor for about five or six hours trying to get an old machine goin'. Took cold in my hip. I been crippled going in the third year. Have to go to the house at night on crutches."

That is not the only misfortune to befall him since his ill-fated attempt for the governorship.

100

"Damn Democrats took my beer license away from me," he says. "After I run for governor. Yes, sir, that was my main biscuits and meat and bread ... The ABC Board closed me up. They claimed they found two open cans of beer on the counter and that I cussed the beer inspector. They put me on welfare, but the welfare won't accept me. I could sure use some, some sort of fare."

R.J. Stansbury is 56. He was reared in Halifax County, "where folks go barefoot," but left the farm to search for work in 1931. "Starvation brought me," he says. He found a job in a Hillsborough cotton mill and worked at it until he opened his store in 1947. He installed septic tanks and did a little plumbing on the side. He was able to quit that when he got his beer license a few years later.

"Sold beer here 12 years and never had no trouble, never called the law the first time. I made a living."

Those were years when the store would often be crowded with people sitting on soft drink crates, benches and broken-down chairs. R.J. would pick his banjo and sing hillbilly songs, closing each by saying, "Thank you, friends." The conversation often turned to politics, and it was from one of those sessions that R.J. got the idea to run for governor.

But now the customers are gone like his beer license, and so are R.J.'s political aspirations.

"I don't see no point in runnin' again," he says. "In fact, I didn't have the filing fee. My creditors might not like it if I run."

He takes up his banjo and begins to pick and sing a song. "Thank you, friends," he says when he finishes, although I am the only one present.

He grins and begins to recall his '64 campaign. One of the highlights of it was his debate with another candidate, Bozo Burleson, who was running on a platform of legalizing gambling and liquor, a platform he later renounced after being "saved" in a born-again religious experience. The debate was billed as "The Great Debate" and it was held on the courthouse steps in Charlotte.

R.J. laughs at the memory. "Bozo had a hell of a big hole in the seat of his britches. I just wished a thousand times I'd told Bozo to turn around back'ards and take a bow to the people behind him. The whole seat of his damn britches was out. If I'd just told 'im that I'd a been *right*."

He plunks on the banjo. "You know, I still feel I'd make a good governor ..." And as he picked in accompaniment, he fell into a little campaign spiel. "Howdy, friends. I certainly am glad to be here with y'all in nineteen hundred and sixty eight. I guess a lot of you remember me in nineteen and sixty four when the old boy was on the campaign trail. Well, this is yours truly, Ol' R.J. Stansbury, the banjo picker, candidate for governor, nineteen and sixty four, and I'm goina sing y'all folks a song. I hope y'all enjoy it . . ."

February, 1968
Hillsborough, North Carolina

Bob Welch
Gold Miner

Even if you are brazen enough to venture past the battery of signs — *Posted! No Trespassing! Keep Out! Enter At Your Own Risk!* — and follow the narrow lane down through the trees and undergrowth, it is unlikely you will be willing to tempt the dogs.

They are a pack of mongrels, ugly, scarred, snarling, fighting amongst themselves when there are no better prospects.

I wait in the car until Bob Welch comes out of the log cabin yelling at the dogs. The dogs back away under his assault, still snarling, turning on one another.

"That's Ding," Bob says of the leader of the pack. "Everybody else is not Ding."

Bob is expecting me, and in deference to my status as a guest, he is not wearing the pistol he usually packs on his hip. ("People never did fool with my father," he later explains about the pistol. "He carried a gun practically all the time. It just came down through the family, I reckon.")

Bob is 74, a tall, lean, grizzled man, with a stubby beard and a touch of mischief in his eyes. He lives alone in a pocket of wild growth, individuality and obstinance, surrounded by expensive new houses on subdivided lots, the leading tendrils of Charlotte's kudzu-like growth.

"I was back here by myself," he says with a contemptuous grunt, "till these damn development hoodlums came along."

Bob calls his cabin the Old Miner's Shack and lists its address as 8016 Poverty Road, although street signs indicate the name of the road is actually Potter's. "Yeah," he says with a little grin, "I named this road up here. State Highway ain't got a thing to do with it. I'll call my road what I want."

He started building his one-room cabin in the trees in 1946, using handsaws to cut the logs. He never quite got it finished, but it doesn't really matter. It's comfortable for him.

"Come on in," he says, pushing open the door, then yelling as a dog tries to slip unnoticed into the clutter inside. "I ain't much of a cook and a whole lot less of a housekeeper."

We sit on hard chairs by the stove, close by a big cardboard box in which a flock of young guineas chirps softly in the warmth of a lightbulb. Bob, who is also called Skip, Pop, Robby and Robin,

103

rummages through the clutter and comes up with a bottle of 100-proof straight rye whiskey.

He plunks it onto the makeshift table between us, and after we each have poured a little snort, Bob reaches again for the bottle. "Let's put the cap back on this thing. If that'd turn over and spill, I'd have a heart attack."

We have not met previously, but Bob has invited me out because we have an old, mutual friend. For a while we talk about our friend, then I turn the subject to Bob. He, in turn, swings it to his own favorite subject: gold mining.

The land on which we sit was once part of a tract of more than 600 acres that Bob's father, Capt. R.L. Welch bought around the turn of the century. The Davis mine, a Civil War-era gold mine, was on the property, and his father mined it profitably for a while. The last attempt to mine it was made in the '30s, when the land was leased to a New Jersey company. Only 40 acres remain in the family now, and Bob owns 10 of them. Three old mining shafts, deep, overgrown depressions, are on his land.

From childhood, Bob yearned to be a gold miner himself. As a young man, he went West and prospected along the Colorado River. But he found no gold, returned home to Matthews and took up electrical work.

"I tell you, the mining just about went to hell down over the years, and there wasn't any way to get a job in it," he says.

From 1931 to 1946, he was manager of Duke Power's Matthews branch. Then he traveled the East Coast as a union electrician on industrial jobs. But he never gave up the dream of gold mining.

When the Howie Mine near Waxhaw was reopened in 1954, he wired it and lived at the mine for a while helping out. Later, he and several partners tried unsuccessfully to reopen a mine near Bessemer City.

Seven years ago, Bob gave up electrical work and retreated to his cabin with his dogs, his chickens, his dreams of gold.

"I wouldn't call it retirement," he says. "I thought that carried some money. Quit. Just say quit. Discontinued."

He has made no attempt to get at the gold he knows must be on his land ("This gold's as fine as flour, and you have an awful time saving it."), but he still gets the *California Mining Journal* every month and keeps up with the price of gold every day.

"I do just as damn little as I can get by with," he says. "Feed the chickens, set up here and listen to the radio, see what kind of bullshit they blowing about, get out, walk around, go up here to the Old Timers Rest (a tavern). I never was a lonesome type person. I always could find something to do. I'm about six months behind in my reading right now."

At night sometimes, his cronies come to drink, laugh, make music, talk about gold and curse the ever-encroaching developers.

Outside, Bob points through the trees to show me a big new house built close against his property.

"I'm just going to pick up and go to Colorado if they get *too* tight," he says.

June, 1979
Matthews, North Carolina

Alex Cockman
Hunter

It was the next-to-last day of hunting season, one of those rare, sparkling winter days, not a cloud in sight. The warm afternoon sun invited lazing in the sweet brown grass. The earth was still winter-damp but not enough to bother.

The hunters, a couple of doctors and a well-to-do photographer from Winston-Salem, were propped against the woodshed behind Alex Cockman's big two-story white farmhouse. Uncle Nate sat on a chopping block. Alex Cockman used a folding lawn chair.

The hunters were telling jokes and laughing and arguing about who had the better dogs. The photographer decided to put on a demonstration of his dogs' superior obedience. He drew belly laughs when the dogs ignored his commands and pleadings in favor of lounging, like the others, in the warm sunshine.

"You're not supposed to laugh at dogs," the photographer snapped. "It'll give 'em an inferiority complex."

"How could you help but laugh?" Uncle Nate said, cackling.

Alex Cockman was enjoying it all. He kept urging Uncle Nate to tell the one about the preacher, which Uncle Nate was slow in warming to but finally did. Alex Cockman sat back and smiled as he told it.

Alex Cockman is a block of granite with a foghorn for a voice. His features are chiseled big and broad. He is 73 and he has spent most of his life doing what he enjoys most: training dogs and hunting. "My daddy came from Gettysburg here on an old horse," he said. "The old horse gave out over here. He just stayed."

As a boy, Alex Cockman roamed the fields and woods of Chatham County learning the land. The experience served him well, because a group of Yankee millionaires had discovered that quail and wild turkey were abundant in Chatham County. They came every winter to shoot them.

By the time he was 13, Alex Cockman was guiding the rich hunters around the countryside, and they soon began leaving their dogs with him for training. That is what he has done for the past 60 years, except for 19 months when he was away in World War I. "I been back here messing and bird hunting ever since," is

106

how he puts it.

In 1922 he built his house and the hunters came and stayed with him in it. After he married Rossner Ferguson and their five sons started coming along, the hunters were relegated to upstairs rooms when they came. Eventually, with the house getting more and more crowded, Alex Cockman built a hunting lodge next to it. The lodge became headquarters for the Hickory Mountain Hunting Club, which at one time boasted 34 members, all rich. The membership included the DuPonts. "Mighty nice people," says Alex. The club leased hunting rights on more than 34,000 acres of land. "Might near all of Alamance and Chatham Counties."

But the rich Yankees gradually died away and now the club is made up of about a dozen doctors, and one photographer, from Winston-Salem. They have leased hunting rights on 7,000 acres.

After Uncle Nate finished his story, the hunters and dogs began to stir. They piled into a stationwagon for the final hunt of the day. The photographer was grumbling that the doctors didn't know how to fix the tailgate properly for the dogs. The doctors were betting whose dog would be sniffing along at the rear of the pack. Uncle Nate, a tall, bony man with a bristly mustache, climbed in with them. He has worked with Alex Cockman most of his life. He would be guiding. He's 80. "Just like a dern squirrel," Cockman said of his friend, grinning. "He's something."

Alex Cockman remained in the chair, petting a brown dog named Tony. "He's the only boy I got now," he said. A cane rested against the chair.

The trouble in his legs started last year but he hunted anyway. "Wore out a jeep," he said. This year the condition grew worse. "Got two or three doctors working on me. Don't know whether they'll cure me or not."

The stationwagon pulled away with the men inside laughing, the dogs looking out the back. Alex Cockman sat and watched them go. For the first time since he went off to the war, Alex Cockman has had to sit out a hunting season.

February, 1968
Siler City, North Carolina

Haskel Gosnel
Top Man

"Just throw it out like a softball," Top Man said, sending the green plastic toy flying through the air toward a stack of soft drink crates, ". . . like *that!*"

Suddenly, he gave the string a flip, catching the top in mid-flight. It jumped back toward him and landed in the palm of his hand, spinning. He let it hop to the back of his other hand for a moment, nudged it back to his palm, then let it walk the string from one hand to the other, a trick so rare and difficult that it isn't even in the book of top tricks.

"Let me try one around behind my back," he said. After he had done that, he spun the top onto the floor, lassoed it with the string and made it leap off the floor into his hand, still spinning. Then he set it dancing across his forehead.

When it comes to tops, Haskel Gosnel is a wizard. There is no trick he can't make them do. Well, that's not exactly true. "I used to catch 'em on my foot," he said, "but I can't do that no more." He could when he was younger, much younger.

"I started spinning a top when I was a kid," he said. "I was about 10 years old, I think it was. When I was almost 12 years old, I started fooling around with baseball and just gave the top up. I quit when I was 12 years old and I didn't have one in my hand again until I was 65."

That was two years ago. Haskel Gosnel, a life-long bachelor, had just retired from his job in a fabric plant in Greenville, South Carolina, where he had been born and lived his whole life. He was passing through a department store one day, and a box of tops caught his eye. "I just bought one. I wanted to see if I could still spin it. I did it the first time."

It didn't take him long to polish up all the tricks he had learned as a boy. In those days, lots of kids spun tops. They would get together, draw a big circle in the dirt and stage top battles. "Just like shootin' marbles. All you could knock out of the ring was yours."

Once he had mastered some of his old tricks again, Haskel Gosnel started carrying the top with him on his regular rounds. He would use it to entertain the boys at the Corner Pockets Billiards parlor, spin it to the delight of children at Henderson's

Curb Market near his home. People began calling him Top Man, and word spread about his expertise.

"I stop uptown where I get on the bus, there'll be people there, they'll ask me, 'Have you got your top?' I'll take it out and start spinning it. Every time I get it out, there'll be a crowd."

The day before, though, he had been embarrassed to be caught at Henderson's Market without a top. He'd had two just a short time earlier, but . . .

"I let this little ol' boy spin one and he hit it on the sidewalk and broke it, got it out of balance, and I just gave it to him." Peanut Delong had the other one. Peanut is his buddy and he'd wanted to learn how to spin one, so Top Man had let him have his last top, and there he was, topless. Tops aren't that easy to come by either. You can't buy them just anywhere. Top Man knows only one store where he can get them, and not even there regularly. So the night before, he had chased all over Greenville looking for Peanut, and when he finally caught up with him, doggone if ol' Peanut hadn't gone and knocked his last top out of balance, too.

But here he was at Henderson's Market again, and there was a crowd as usual and that out-of-balance top was spinning across his forehead and walking the string. "I never have seen nobody could let it run down the string like I do," he said.

But he wasn't satisfied with the performance of this one. "Wish I had a good wood one like they used to have when I was a kid, but I can't find one. You can find some wood ones now once in a while but they're not no good."

He flipped the top toward the bottle crates again and it leapt back instantly, like a yoyo, and sat spinning in his hand. "See, that's easy," he said. "You can learn how to do that in 15 minutes."

July, 1975
Greenville, South Carolina

Alan Hancock
Stew King

Steam curls from the black iron pot imbedded in the belly of the brick furnace. Woodsmoke swirls and drifts down the hill toward the river. It is Friday and Hancock's Stew Foundry is firing up.

"Whenever you get away from a cast iron pot and firing with wood," Alan Hancock says, "you've done got away from the Brunswich stew business."

He is 74, a twinkly-eyed, jowly man who loves to talk. He started cooking stews when he was 10. His "foundry," as he calls it, is just a screened porch tacked onto a small woodworking shop he owns on a hillside overlooking the Smith River in what used to be the town of Spray, now joined with Draper and Leaksville to form Eden.

On the porch sit an old refrigerator, a bench and a big, rough-hewn table with lard tins beneath and pots and dishpans spread over the top. Washtubs hang on a wall, and big, wooden, stew-stirring paddles hang over the furnace.

Hancock's Stew Foundry has been in operation 25 years. It opens the first week in September and closes at Easter. Stew is served only on Saturdays, and people come from all around to get it. Alan Hancock is known as a master stewmaker.

"My stew background began in 1904," he says. "I was just a kid then, of course. My uncle, Robert M. Hancock, was a pioneer stewmaker of Rockingham County. I helped him." The first stew he helped with was at the old ironworks near Reidsville. Claude Kitchen was a candidate for governor and he was there along with a lot of other people. Alan and his uncle fixed 400 gallons of stew, of which not a drop went uneaten.

He was still just a boy when he became a stewmaker on his own; forced into it, he recalls, because his uncle got sick, had a stew to cook, and there was nobody else to cook it.

"He cooked for everybody under the sun that came along," Alan Hancock says of his uncle, "and never charged a cent." That was something the young stewmaker changed. "I got to cooking for everybody in the country just like he did, every church, every PTA . . . then I found out you could sell it. That's when I stopped cooking for everybody and started cooking for myself."

111

Just Folks

The biggest stew he ever cooked was when Melville Broughton was running for governor and a rally was held at a ballpark in Draper. Alan Hancock cooked 600 gallons of stew. It took 35 pots.

Although he has been a stewmaker for most of his life, Alan Hancock made his living as a contractor. "House building mostly. Built some right nice jobs around about." He retired from that nine years ago, but he's still cooking stews.

He cooks once a week at his foundry, starting on Friday because it takes many hours to cook a good stew. He starts with meat — chicken, turkey, beef, pork, squirrel sometimes. Vegetables come later, tomatoes, corn, lima beans. He cooks all night so the stew will be ready Saturday morning.

"Anybody can cook a Brunswick stew," he says. "The secret is seasoning . . ."

He grows his own peppers for that.

On Saturdays, Alan Hancock holds forth at his 64-gallon pot, wearing a paper Pepsi-Cola hat, ladling thick, steaming stew, and talking all the while.

Some of his customers take it in paper cartons to go, some take paper traysful and sit at the big table, spooning stew down with crackers and listening to Alan Hancock.

There was a time, not so long before, when there weren't as many customers as there once had been, and Alan Hancock began to wonder if Brunswick stew might be on the way out. Not anymore. "It's coming back, coming back right good. Some time ago it looked like barbecue was going to step in, you know, but it didn't do it."

He has no plans, at any rate, to abandon his pot anytime soon. "Had it 40 years," he says, stirring the meat beginning to cook in it. "I s'pect it's cooked more'n than a million gallons."

December, 1968
Eden, North Carolina

112

Der Wing Hanson
The Laundryman's Last Day

The little brick-front store was almost empty. It had been swept clean and several worn brooms stood in a row by the back door. The only things remaining now were the counter at the front, an old clock on the wall near the counter, and two calendars. One of the calendars had a colorful picture of a pretty Chinese girl on it. It advertised the Tuck High Company, importers of Chinese goods in New York. The other calendar was from the Hop Kee Restaurant on Mott Street in New York.

The unclaimed items, a big boxful, some of which had been there for years, had been given to a preacher to be taken to somebody who could use them. The shelves and all the equipment were gone, hauled away earlier in the week by a laundry equipment company.

"Just give it away," Der Wing Hanson was saying. "I can't get nobody to give me a penny for it. Just give it away. I can't get a penny for it."

There isn't much demand for old laundry equipment.

Der Wing Hanson leaned against the counter and looked out through the plateglass window. He is not much taller than the counter, a portly, round-faced man whose sleek black hair has turned white at the temples. It was late afternoon, and people were hurrying past outside, rushing home from work. Ordinarily, Der Wing Hanson would have been getting ready to close down his busines for the day and go home himself. No more.

He was about to remove from the window the big piece of cardboard on which he had lettered "Going Out Of Business." He was already out of business. And soon the red paint that spelled out "WHITE STAR LAUNDRY" would be scraped off the window. The building already had been leased. A book and card shop soon would occupy it. Greensboro had lost its last Chinese hand laundry.

It was nearly 44 years since Der Wing Hanson had left Hong Kong and followed his father to Greensboro. He was 18 then. His father operated a laundry in Greensboro and Der Wing worked for him until his father died a few years later. The White Star Laundry was on Market Street then, but 21 years ago Der Wing Hanson bought this little building on Eugene Street and moved

113

the laundry to it. Business was good, but it was never better than during World War II, when so many soldiers were stationed in Greensboro. "In the war time, I have 15 people work for me," he recalled.

Primarily, though, the White Star Laundry served the downtown businessmen, the bankers and lawyers and insurance executives who needed a freshly starched white shirt every day and wanted them done right. That was Der Wing Hanson's specialty. Shirts. He never had dry cleaning equipment. He didn't do much other laundry. Just shirts. He did them by hand, taking great care with each one.

Most of his customers were regulars, but over the years their numbers gradually diminished. Der Wing Hanson would stand behind the counter each day greeting his customers with a smile; there were enough of them to keep him and his wife, Lee Mee Sing, busy. But in the last few years things had changed drastically, until finally Der Wing Hanson didn't see how he could go on any longer.

"Business about give out," he said. "That's all. Yeah, business had been good I keep open here. But business bad." He shrugged. "You can't make a living, you got to close."

And that was what he did. The White Star Laundry had been done in by DripDri and PermaPrest and the automatic washer. But there are some who regret the passing, and they have told Der Wing Hanson so. "I got lots of old friends come in here, some come in here 15, 20 years. Everybody ask me, 'What I'm going to do with my shirts now? I can't take it to the other laundry. They always mess and tear up.' But I don't know . . ."

I asked him if he were sad about having to close, and he said, "What you mean, sad?"

"You know, hurt inside."

His young son, who had been standing nearby listening explained in Chinese. Der Wing Hanson looked quickly away, then down. "Oh, I can't tell that," he said. "It's all right, I guess. I'm doing a long time, see. All my good friends are sorry. I am too, but . . ."

May, 1973
Greensboro, North Carolina

Pompey Cardwell
Roger-Dodger

First comes the secret handshake, an intricate four-part maneuver. It ends with an okay sign, a whistle and the chant: "Roger-Dodger, Mac-Pete. Skin-a-rootbeer, Sarge. If you're ever down a well, ring my bell. If you're ever up a tree, call on me. If you're ever in a jam, here I am. Which way they went? Straight up and down. Rah-h-h-ger-Dodger!" Somewhere in there are a couple of clicks done from the corner of the mouth. With that, you are inducted. You have entered the Royal Order of Roger-Dodgers.

The international headquarters of the Roger-Dodgers is in a small room tucked into one side of the old and crumbling New Brick Tobacco Warehouse, where the exalted leader, Pompey Cardwell, lives. At mid-day, he is asleep on a quilt-topped bed in the cluttered room. Roused from his nap, he sits on the side of the bed and wipes the sleep from his eyes.

"How you doin'?" he says with a grin. "Rah-h-h-ger-Dodger!"

The Roger-Dodgers are on every wall, kids smiling down from school pictures and snapshots pasted into frames, hundreds of them. Pompey smiles back at them. "They all little Roger-Dodgers," he says. "I always put 'em on the wall, hang 'em up. Some of 'em's done got married on me, got some more little Roger-Dodgers."

Out across the hills and hollows of northwestern North Carolina and part of southwestern Virginia, lots of people know Pompey Cardwell, know him to be a certified character who answers to Pompey, or Mac-Pete, or Roger-Dodger, or Sarge, or whatever name people choose to call him. If they don't know him, there is a chance they may have heard of some of his wild exploits, a few of which are legendary.

Pompey is showing his age at 61. He is slump-shouldered, paunchy. His face looks as if he has just awakened. He begins to explain about the Roger-Dodgers. "Oh, it's just a little something 'other everybody likes, I guess . . ."

It began years ago when Pompey was a lifeguard at Fairystone Park in Virginia. He had a swimming class full of kids and he thought the group ought to have a name, so why not Roger-Dodger? Besides, he always had trouble remembering names so

115

he just called everybody Roger-Dodger or Mac-Pete to simplify matters.

Anyway, it grew from that. The handshake evolved, followed by the chant, and little Roger-Dodgers began cropping up all around. Pompey got around; he liked kids, and he made Roger-Dodgers of all he met.

Now, whenever he goes driving through the country, or gets into his boat for a twirl around the lake, he'll pass a house and toot his horn and kids will run out giving the okay sign and shouting "RAH-H-H-H-GER-DODGER!" It never fails to give him a chuckle.

He collects their pictures and puts them on the wall. Every year he gathers up a big group, hooks up his boat to a tractor, and they climb into the boat and ride in the Madison Christmas parade, Roger-Dodgering everybody in sight. Until they got too expensive, Pompey passed out Roger-Dodger t-shirts to members.

The movement has spread as members grew older. There have been Roger-Dodger chapters in Germany, Korea, Vietnam. A Roger-Dodger basketball team formed in Chapel Hill. "Yeah, we got em all over the whole country, the world," says Pompey, chuckling. Membership is for a lifetime and each year the older members get together with Pompey for a reunion.

On a table in his room rests a stack of new pictures. Pompey shuffles through them. "Here's some I got to put up," he says. "There's that little girl hugged my neck out there a while ago. When I die, I'm going to give her $5, or something . . . Yessir, this is the headquarters of the little Roger-Dodgers. We got a old Skipper-loo dog around here somewhere. He's the head man of the Roger-Dodgers. He's *some* dog. Where's old Skipper?"

Skipper is the mascot of the Roger-Dodgers and at official gatherings he is dressed up in a hat and glasses and a pipe. Skipper is also Pompey's faithful companion and servant. Whenever Pompey gets a little thirst, which is fairly regularly, he just calls Skip and tells him about it. Skip heads out of the warehouse and trots down the street to the poolroom. When the bartender sees him coming, he puts a cold one in a paper sack and has it waiting when Skip arrives. Skip promptly delivers it to Pompey. This keeps Pompey from having to get out of bed or interrupt his story telling when he is in the warehouse at market time.

On a recent day, some of the boys at the poolroom decided to play a trick on Pompey and put an empty can in the sack. Pompey laughs. "I said, 'Skip, what you doin'? You done drunk that beer!' Skip looked up at me, he said, 'You know I don't drink.' Back down the street he went."

At the mention of his name, Skip comes nosing into the room. "There's old Skipper-loo," Pompey says. "He's the head man of the Roger-Dodgers. Come here, Skip. What you doin' old buddy-buddy . . . He's 18 months old. I picked him up on the street down yonder when he was a pup. Somebody kicked him out, had icicles on him when I picked him up. That rascal slept with me about four days . . ."

As usual, a crowd gathers around Pompey. Grizzled characters, red-faced, most wearing overalls, wander into the room, and soon they are hooting and howling as Pompey tells again the stories of his wild exploits. "Mac-Pete, tell the one about the time . . ."

A woman from the warehouse office passes by and sticks her head in to say, "Pompey, those girls in the office were still excited about you losing your britches over there the other day. They really liked those red polka-dot shorts."

That's another story, of course. Pompey tells all about it. He was doing his famous Roger-Dodger camel walk for the enlightenment of some of the boys during one of the sales and his pants collapsed on him, right in front of the office window. The women in the office threatened to charge him with indecent exposure. "Them little bitty skirts *they* wear and they going to charge *me!*" Pompey says with mock indignation.

It goes on like that, story after story, everybody laughing and having a high old time, and then Pompey says, "Skip, go get us something to drink." Skip jumps up, heads out the door and down the street. He is back shortly, carrying a cold beer in a paper sack between his teeth. Pompey takes the beer and pats Skip on the head.

"You a good boy, Skip. Wudn't for you, don't know what I'd do. I'd starve to death. Rah-h-h-h-ger-Dodger, Mac-Pete, skin-a-rootbeer, Sarge!" And he laughs.

November, 1971
Madison, North Carolina

Paul Swanson
Mobile Lawyer

It has been another morning without success. No jobs. So Paul Swanson leaves Iredell County's shiny new Hall of Justice and, taking a shortcut through the yard of a nearby house, walks back across Davie Street.

"Won't you step into my office?" he says with a smile as he opens the driver's door of his Volkswagen camper-van. The van is a '69 model. Faded red. It sports a "God Is My Co-Pilot" sign on the front. Small American flags fly from the tops of both front doors. Gold letters on the rear side windows proclaim Paul Swanson to be a lawyer and notary public. So does a big signboard propped against the bumper.

"I have been practicing now starting my 47th year," he says, settling himself behind the steering wheel, "and this is one of my philosophies here." He indicates a plastic placard on the dashboard. It says, "Don't regret growing old. It's a privilege denied to many." Paul Swanson is 74, a soft-spoken, courtly man. On this morning, he is wearing a red and black bow tie. The buttons of his multi-colored sportcoat are fastened. The pockets bulge with notepads and pens. A red rosebud is wilting in his lapel. His white hair is covered by a yellow rain hat with the brim pulled down all around. "This is my card," he says, taking a business card from his pocket.

Even as a boy back in Wilkes County, Paul Swanson knew he wanted to be a lawyer. "I was reared in the Wilkesboro courtyard almost," he explains, "and I observed the old-time lawyers . . . and thought I'd like to be like one of them." He attended Guilford College, then switched to High Point College where he graduated in 1928. After a short stint as a teacher in Lexington, he went off to law school at Duke. He stayed a year, didn't like it and transferred to Wake Forest. After one semester there he took the bar exam and passed.

His first practice was in High Point, where his family had moved. He later returned to Wilkesboro, found that he was unable to build a practice there and went on to Winston-Salem. In 1939, he moved to Sparta, where he practiced until 1965 when he and his wife, Ina, moved to her family homeplace at the one-way bridge on Big Hunting Creek in Iredell County, 19 miles from

Statesville. "I attempted to retire and backed out," he says with a chuckle. "Well, my wife put me to plantin' flowers and workin' for Honey-Do. You know, Honey do this and Honey do that."

He rented an upstairs office in an old building in Statesville and was back in the law business. But in 1971 he had a heart attack and his doctor advised him to get rid of his office with its 32 steps to climb. That was when he got the idea for an office on wheels. He bought the Volkswagen van, outfitted it with a battered typewriter and a big office chair, and he was back in business.

"I kindly got the idee from a story I read about some lawyers in Los Angeles rented a lot and brought campmobiles there. They all camped there in the day and they went home in the evening."

Paul Swanson's van is no luxury office. It is crowded, cluttered with papers and old law books. A red bandana is tied around the steering column. An aging wind-up alarm clock ticks on the dashboard. The folded rear seat serves as a desktop. The kerosene space heater that squats between the two front seats has thoroughly smoked the ceiling. The drinking fountain is a plastic milk jug filled with water.

On weekday mornings, Paul Swanson drives his van to town and parks it in the driveway of Anderson Nash's house on Davie Street. "I've been a-parkin' here in this gentleman's yard for four or five years," he says. Nash charges him nothing for the privilege. After he puts out his signboard, Paul Swanson heads to the Hall of Justice for the calling of the court docket. "Each morning I attend to that, pick up a case now and then."

If there are no jobs, he returns to his van to wait for any clients who might happen by. Those who come are invited to take the passenger seat to discuss their business. The seat is seldom occupied. "I just have a small amount of business," he says. "Just last week I had a fraud case on food stamps. She came here. She knew where I parked. I got her a chance to be on probation so she could pay off what was due. I've averaged two or three cases a month, active in the courtroom. Then I write wills, deeds of trust, what have you. People are beginning to learn me by the vehicle. Seems like it's sort of a trademark that they know. I've been criticized by some for it, and others look at it and wonder why. Main reason why is the rent's cheaper. I'm trying to beat the high rent."

He remains on call in his van until 3 each afternoon, usually reading while he waits. "You might say I've been an extensive reader," he says, smiling. "Still trying to read everything I can, keeping up with what's going on in the world." Sometimes he

119

justs rests. "I have a sleeping bag. Yeah, I can crawl up there and take a nap, sleep between customers."

He used to bring his dog with him for company, but the dog got run over and was killed. For a while after that he brought one of the dog's puppies, but that didn't work out. "He ate my curtains," he says, motioning toward the shredded remains still hanging in evidence on the windows. "Ate wills. That dog had no respect for documents."

May, 1977
Statesville, North Carolina

Clyde Williams
Old-Time Fiddler

"See, I was born and raised on a mill hill," Clyde Williams said, "and this is a fact. In the summertime, you know, people would set out on their porches and turn their radios on real loud. You could walk down a mill hill or ride a bicycle down by the houses on a Saturday night and every house you passed would have the Grand Ol' Opry on. Oh, the Opry was *it*."

That was in the '30s, and the signal from radio station WSM in Nashville had just reached the hills of North Carolina around Newton, where Clyde Williams grew up. The Opry was different then. The solemn ol' judge, George T. Hay, presided. To identify the Opry, he blew on wooden whistles that sounded like steamboat whistles. The popular groups on the show were the Possum Hunters, the Gully Jumpers.

"The Grand Ol Opry used to be a monopoly," Clyde Williams said. "It was built purely on old-time music. It started out and stayed for over 20 years as a program that had nothing but fiddle music. They had the best fiddle players in the world. If you heard the Opry all the way through, you would hear at least 45 fiddle tunes."

That fiddle music did something to Clyde Williams. From the time he was seven, he'd wanted a fiddle. His father, who played guitar and mandolin, said no; he'd have to learn guitar and play it in fiddle bands first. By the time he was 13, Clyde had mastered the guitar without lessons. The next year, his father bought him a $12 fiddle in Charlotte.

He learned to play that fiddle by listening to the Opry. "As soon as I heard a tune I wanted to learn, I'd go back in another room and work on it. It was fairly easy for me to pick up." His favorites were the Possum Hunters. He loved their music and worked hard to reproduce it. By the time he was 19, he was good enough to be invited to join a touring professional group. He turned it down.

"I felt like the lifestyle was just . . . see, I've always stayed at home pretty close, never liked to do any traveling."

He soon was traveling anyway. The Army got him. But it gave him a chance he had long dreamed about. While he was stationed in Kentucky in 1945, he slipped down to Nashville and saw the solemn ol' judge and the Possum Hunters on the Opry. It was a memorable experience for him, for the Opry was about to change.

"To me, the Grand Ol' Opry was done away with in 1945," he said. "They started pushin' out the fiddle music. They started pushin' it out in the autumn of '45 and the solemn ol' judge stopped blowing that whistle the night they started pushin' it out."

On a crudely built table in the front room of Clyde Williams' small house in Coulwood, a Charlotte suburb, several wooden whistles are arrayed. Box whistles. Two channel whistles. Three channel whistles. All replicas of the whistles the solemn ol' judge used on the Grand Ol' Opry. Clyde Williams made them. "I'm a person who likes to dream of things gone by," he said with a smile, "live in a fantasy world. I guess I'm trying to dodge reality, I don't know. The Grand Ol' Opry meant so much to me I'm just tryin' to keep these things alive."

Really the whistles are symbols of a dream. For more than 30 years, Clyde Williams has been struggling to keep alive the old-time music he used to hear on the Opry. He has been steadily losing ground. Through the years, he has played the old-time music at fiddlers' conventions and square dances, but he has found it harder and harder to find other musicians to play his style of music with him. "There's a lot of styles of old-time music, but according to my knowledge, I'm the only one playing this kind of music in this area anymore. I pretty well stand alone in my style of music."

His style is that of the Possum Hunters. It requires a guitar, a particular type of banjo playing. For the past couple of years, Clyde Williams has played little because he hasn't been able to find other musicians to make up a group. "I'm a perfectionist," he says. "If I'm playin', I don't want no flaws in it."

He hasn't quit trying, though. "You take a person that loves old-time music, they love it with everything they got. It's kind of a religion to me." In his mind, he still rides down the mill hill on his bicycle on a summer Saturday night and everybody is listening to fiddle music on the Grand Ol' Opry.

"The public has not changed that much. I believe people really love old-time music, but they just don't get it. WSM was the only place that had it, and when they stopped it, we just didn't have it no more. You know, people way back, they didn't know everything, but a lot of what they had was really worth keeping. I think it's pathetic that we've lost some of these things. I'd love to see something done for some of this lost music. I swear I would, and I could do it if I could get a chance.

"I would give anything if I could get an hour on a radio somewhere. If I could get an hour on a radio station, I believe I could get somebody and train 'em up and play this kind of music. I honestly believe it would be the most popular thing on the radio. I believe the people are just like they were back then. People all want happiness. We all want it, and this lively music represents happiness. I don't think you can get that out of the human heart."

February, 1978
Charlotte, North Carolina

Joe Crosson
Tattoo Artist

He rattles around in an old, blue Cadillac, his tresses flying in the wind, and usually there'll be four or five dogs bouncing around the seats. A mud flap hanging from the rear bumper lets all know who's driving. Tattoo Joe.

Tattoo Joe Crosson is 34, a native of Union Cross, which is halfway between High Point and Winston-Salem. His tattoo parlor is on Highway 311. It used to be a beer joint and dance hall but then there was the shootout (the bloodstains are still on the floor, the clock on the wall pocked with bullet holes) and the authorities forced it to close. So Tattoo Joe moved in. He set up his tattooing equipment behind the bar and moved in a lot of pinball machines that sit and blink. Lots of unusual things decorate the walls: a Hell's Angels poster, several sets of deer antlers, a nice rack from a moose, a hornet's nest, a stuffed sloth permanently sleeping in the traditional sloth position on a piece of tree limb. A mannequin's torso with an eagle and flag tattooed on it stands near the bar. A sign advises, "No Drunks or Obscene Work Tattooed Here."

There is also a chart of tattoo designs and prices. How about a nice skull and crossbones? Maybe a dagger with entwined snake? The most expensive is only $18.

Dogs of many breeds roam about the parlor. Joe raises and sells them as a sideline. He sits now on a stool by the bar looking for all the world like a dark-haired Buffalo Bill. His hair is wavy and hangs well below the shoulders. His mustache is big and curled on the ends. His red goatee looks as if it might have been lifted from the chin of some ancient Chinese sage. "I didn't grow it to be a hippie or anything," he says. "I had it when I was the only one."

He's had long hair for 12 years, except for a brief period when he was clean-shaven and had a flattop. That just didn't work. People said he looked too young to be a tattoo artist. They didn't want a child standing over them with a needle.

Actually, Joe is a tattoo artist only part of the year. The rest of the time he's on the road as a carnival sideshow performer. "On the shows," he says, "they call me a man who drives nails in my

head. I drive spiked nails in my nose. A 16-penny nail, I can completely hide it. It goes straight back. I stick hatpins in my arms,
pull 'em all the way through, a human pin cushion, you know."

He also does a human robot act and sucks his belly in so it looks
as if it has disappeared. He used to eat fire. He had to give that up
for the sake of his hair and whiskers. Fire eating was okay but he
did not want to be a human torch.

Joe started out to be a welder, but he quickly decided he did not
want to do that all his life. He wanted to travel. So when he was
16 he joined a carnival. It was with the carnival that he picked up
tattooing. The show's tattoo artist got drafted. He owed money to
the show's owner. He couldn't pay. The owner took his equipment in payment and, in turn, offered it to Joe, who took it. Joe
had never tattooed anybody, but he'd watched the tattoo artist
work. He figured he could do it. He practiced on carnival people.
His first job as a professional was to put "Airborne" across some
guy's chest in Oklahoma. He's been at it since. He has put as many
as 35 tattoos on one man. he has tattooed identification marks on
babies, medical information on patients. But the tattoo business is
not exactly booming nowadays, he says, at least not in these
parts. "Sometimes I don't put a tattoo on in a month."

Joe is particular about whom he tattoos. He doesn't like to tattoo
somebody unless that person already has tattoos, or unless he is
convinced the person sincerely wants a tattoo. "If a person gets a
tattoo because they want it, they'll never regret it, but if they get
one because their buddy talked them into it, or because
somebody dared 'em, they'll always regret it. A tattoo is nothing
really to be proud of, but if you like it, I don't think anybody else
ought to be able to tell you it's no good. A lot of people say you
ain't supposed to get it because it says something about it in the
Bible, about marking your body . . . I don't believe that's what it
means. To me, I believe a tattoo is not going to keep anybody
from going to heaven. It's not just your low class people that get
tattoos, you know."

A lot of women get tattoos, he says. They favor small roses,
birds and butterflies, and they usually get them on breasts and
buttocks, often at the instigation of husbands. "I don't make a
habit of tattooing women," says Joe, "but if it's a nice-looking
woman, I'll tattoo her, because I figure she knows what she's doing. A girl can take a tattoo easier than a guy. A woman's mind is
stronger when it comes to pain. Pain is in your mind, you know.
Some guys, even before you touch them with a needle, they're
sweating."

125

Just Folks

Joe has two tattoos himself, one on each shoulder, for balance. He has a rose on one shoulder and a heart and dagger with rose and bird on the other. "But I don't especially like tattoos," he says. "I got these when I first started to tattoo. I figured a tattoo artist ought to have tattoos."

Even though he doesn't care much for tattoos himself, Joe has taken on a sense of obligation to the art. "The old tattoo artists are dying and there's nobody to take their place," he says. "These guys who want tattoos got nobody to go to to get it done right, so they do it theirself, and they end up with a bunch of chain gang tattoos. I don't think there's anything looks worse than chain gang tattoos."

March, 1970
Union Cross, North Carolina

Red Ballard
The Old Vaudevillian

Red Ballard looked up and grinned. "Still can," he said. It was obvious he'd like nothing better than to hop up from the couch and do a buck and wing. "Course, I can't on account of my back. But I still know how."

Big Red is what his friends call him. He is just that, tall with a big belly and a bulbous, Jimmy Durante-like nose. His red hair has faded and is slowly going. He's 64. A cigar protruded from the corner of his mouth. "Used to use a cigar for a prop," he said, taking it from his mouth and waving it in the air. "I been in and out of show business 40-some years."

Vaudeville. Not big-time vaudeville, but vaudeville nevertheless. "After vaudeville died, some of the oldtimers made the big time," Red was saying. "I never did. Lot of 'em made big money. Lot of 'em ended up like me, didn't make nothing."

He was a boy in Mt. Gilead when show business fever set in. It never subsided. At 11, he got his first taste taking tickets at the Saturday night shows held every week in the town's schoolhouse. At 12, he could do a buck and wing and mimic the comics. He was 16 when he moved to Thomasville with his mother and nine brothers and sisters. He went to work in a hosiery mill boarding socks. It took him two years to get back to show business, but he made it when he landed a nighttime and weekend job as usher and stagehand at the old Palace Theater on Salem Street.

The Palace was on the Joe Spiegelburg show circuit and the shows came for three days each week. They were always the same, a couple of black-face comics and five or six Gandy dancers, as the chorus girls were called. Red loved it.

When the Palace's stage manager quit, Red moved into the job. He recalls one of the Palace's amateur nights when a young man named Kay Kyser came from Chapel Hill and entered. "He did a dern good job. I remember it well. He's a good hoofer." Red liked the amateur nights best of all, because he entered them himself, repeating routines he'd picked up from other comics. One day a black-face comic named Benny Kirkland told him, "Red, you've got the makings of a good comic." Red couldn't remember ever

127

hearing sweeter words. One weekend he slipped off to Anderson, South Carolina, where he performed with Kirkland at the old Opera House, his face smeared with burnt cork paste (Stein's Makeup Company, Cincinnati, Ohio, $1.25 a pound).

He was 21 when he quit his theater job and hit the road, working first in the tent shows. "That was $12 a week and your keep." He rode in a T-Model Truck, pulling a cookhouse, and he played towns like Albemarle, Troy, Star, Candor, Rockingham, Ellerbe. "All small towns, admission 30¢." He was called Dusty then, a black-face comic.

He laughed at the memory. "A 10-minute monologue cost you $2.50. A script bill cost you $5. There were some good ones. 'Long Distance Telephone.' 'Sit Down, Ham.' 'Over The River, Charlie.' Oh, just a bunch of 'em."

He made several tours with the tent shows, spent six weeks with a medicine show, then moved into theaters in slightly larger towns. But he had got into vaudeville at the wrong time. Talking pictures came out and vaudevile began to die.

"You'd catch a show, maybe stay out a month, two months, maybe not," he recalled. It was no way to keep a wife and children fed. Red moved to Greensboro. He worked in the paint business. He traveled selling socks and fountain pens. He worked in a clothing store, sold cars, tended bar. He took shows when he could get them. Once he worked two weeks with a carnival girlie show but he didn't like it. He tried to stay close to show business, doing promotion work for theaters, hanging out in projection booths. For a while he did a clown act. But it was over, and he knew it. Vaudeville was dead and so was his show business career.

In recent years, his health has not been good. He has done only two shows in the past two years, both in smoky, roughneck dance halls. "You can't do comedy in a dance hall," he said. "They don't want to listen to a comic get up there and blow off. They want to dance and have fun."

From one of the joints, there had been at least a little satisfaction. "I understand it's closed now," Red said with a grin. "Maybe I closed it."

July, 1968
Greensboro, North Carolina

128

Dan Melton
Tenant Farmer

Gilley said he was around back in the "tater patch," so I went around and found him lying on his belly in the hay, digging sweet potatoes from one of his teepee-like potato hills.

I sat beside him in the cold winter sunshine, and as he worked and I pulled cockleburrs from my socks and pants legs, we talked about hilling potatoes and growing collards and other important things.

He was farming only an acre or two now, he said, in little patches here and there — he was, after all, getting on in years, soon to be 75 — but it was enough.

"Grow more'n I can eat," he said with a little grin. "I'm going to sell these sweet taters."

I asked how long he'd been on this place.

"The 22nd day of March coming, I'll be here 48 years."

He had come, he said, from a place near Jefferson, South Carolina, where he'd grown up on a farm, the son of a sharecropper. After he married Gilley, he'd become a sharecropper himself, he and Gilley living with her people.

"To tell you the truth, I don't hardly know what caused me to take a notion to come up here," he said. "But I had a brother-in-law here. And my wife — after her daddy died, wasn't nobody but us — she couldn't be satisfied, seemed like."

His brother-in-law gave them a place to stay, just across the field from where they now live. "He was mighty good to me. Let me work his stock, raise me something to eat. I lived purty good. Money, I didn't know what that was."

Eventually, he bought himself a team of horses, working off the asking price with the man who owned them, and set about farming rented land, growing cotton. But it wasn't easy going.

"Them was Hoover times, you know. I know you heard old people talk about Hoover times. I tell you, he was some dude. If he'd been president up to now, they wouldn't be nobody but him. The rest of us would've been starved to death.

"Course, I made it all right. I come out from that. When it come time to vote Hoover out, you know, they voted him out. And Roosevelt, President Roosevelt, he got in, and he was an awful good man." A tabby cat was rubbing against him as he stretched

129

to reach into the tater hill. "Scat from here, ol' cat!" he said, pushing the cat away.

"He tried to look out for poor people and he did. He *made* jobs fer 'em. Called WPA, PWA, something like that. He didn't give anything away. You had to work for it. I worked in that mess four or five year. Rollin' wheelbar's, bustin' rocks, everything else. Worked in a rock quarry. You know where that big rock quarry is back over there near Linwood? I holp make that big hole. We was making 90 cents a day."

He held up a sweet potato he'd just pulled out of the hay. That there's where you can tell they're keepin' good. See them little sprouts? He ain't thinkin' about rottenin', is he?"

He carefully examined each potato before putting it into the bushel basket that sat between us. The basket was filling slowly as we talked. The subject turned to his health.

Except for the measles, he said, he'd only been sick once in his life, laid up for a week during the flu epidemic that hit right after World War I.

"Just don't get sick," he said. "I bet I've took the least medicine of anybody in the world for my age. Nothin' just don't bother me. I tell you what I think helps me more than anything else, just what you seen me doing yestiddy."

I had met him the day before. He was riding his bicycle to the store. "Ride it every day somewhere or other," he said. "That's the best exercise you can get. I wouldn't do without a bicycle."

Finally, the basket was full. Dan Melton pushed the hay back inside the hill and closed it, moving slowly and methodically. We went up to the house then and sat on blocks he had sawed from a huge dead oak that had fallen in the yard.

"Oh, yeah," he said, "I've had a good life. Wished I could go back over it. You know, if I had mine to go over again, and I knowed like I know now, I could've been the richest man they was in this part of the country.

"I had a chance buying all this land in here, 500 acres of land in here for $15,000. I said, 'Good gracious alive, if a man had that much money . . .' "

Much of that land now fronts on High Rock Lake and is lined with vacation houses. The owner had offered to sell it to Dan Melton on time.

"But I had a houseful of children and I was just scared to take a chance," he said. "The way things picked up, I coulda paid fer it. Shucks, I'da paid it off just as easy as fallin' off this block."

"You'd've been a millionaire now," I said.

"Yeah, but I wouldn't felt a bit bigger than I do right now. Naw, if I'da bought it, I'd been right where I am now."

He pays no rent on the weathered, decaying, rusty-roofed house where he and Gilley have lived for 48 years, a house made famous in a painting by artist Bob Timberlake, who has a studio just across the pasture. Timberlake also painted a portrait of Dan Melton and included it in a book of his paintings.

"There's one thing I've always done," Dan was saying. "I ain't never lived nothin' but a honest life. I try to serve the Lord. That's the only thing a poor man's got. He can get that free and that's about all he can get, and it's worth the most of anything he *can* get."

December, 1979
Southmont, North Carolina

Charlie Stafford
Blacksmith

Things don't change much around Charlie Stafford's place on Bunker Hill Road. He still lives in a 180-year-old house he bought in 1912 and fixed up for his family. The house was once a hotel and stagecoach stop. Many years ago, long before he bought the house, Charlie rode the stagecoach past it himself.

"I went on it from Asheboro to a little place over near Stokesdale they call Egypt," he says.

Traces of the old stagecoach road are still there in his yard, and it was squarely in the center of that old road that he chose to set his blacksmith shop. About the only thing that has changed around Charlie's blacksmith shop in the past half century is Charlie. He's gotten considerably older in all that time, but at age 85, he still goes to work in the shop every day, Sundays often included.

On a hot August afternoon, he is dressed as he always is, winter and summer, in overalls with a heavy, long-sleeve work shirt buttoned at the collar and a battered old hat. He has just finished repairing a gate on a cattle trailer, and now he has turned his attention to putting a new handle on a hammer. "Feller brought it last night and wanted me to put a handle on it," he says, pausing to spit tobacco juice at the earth floor, "and I told him I'd do it today when I got ready."

He makes the hammer handles himself, just as he makes handles for many other tools, hewing them with an ax from logs of ash or hickory, shaping them with drawknife and plane. "I made 391 ax handles since the 16th day of November a year ago. I made 120 little hammer handles and 126 sledgehammer handles like them hanging over there." The charge for an ax handle is $2, plus another quarter for affixing it. He figures he's coming out at that. He's never believed in robbing his customers.

"They's folks come here and say, 'You old-fashioned,' " he says with a chuckle. "I say, 'I wish to God there was more of 'em.' Half the fellers I do work for give me a heap more than I charge 'em. Always have."

He usually grins and tells them he isn't worth what he charges. "I don't need much," he says. "If I can make a dollar a day I can get by. I'm like Will Rogers. I grow what I eat and eat what I

133

grow."

Charlie never set out to be a blacksmith. He wanted to farm. "Still rather farm than anything there is to do. I grow a little wheat, oats, corn, hay. Used to raise tobacco." Circumstances caused him to get into smithing. "I got into it and didn't aim to. I just got in it 'cause I could buy the tools for $20. I thought it would be worth that. I been messin' with this stuff ever since 19 and 19. Fifty-seven years will be the 28th of September. That's when I bought the tools. Bought 'em from a feller Henry Sechriest in High Point. Bought a bellows, a anvil, a vise, all kinds of old stuff. Just all grades of tongs. Nowadays you take 90 per cent of the fellers don't know what a set of tongs is.

"I learned it for myself. My granddaddy was a blacksmith, my granddaddy Stafford, and my uncle was a blacksmith, Uncle Gene. By the time I come along, my granddaddy had done quit. He was too old. He didn't live to be but 97, seven months and 17 days. I did go up to Kernersville a time or two and watch old man Bob Stewart on bad days. They wasn't many as good as J.R. Stewart. I got this bellows here from him. I wore the old bellows down and I got a chance to get this one here from him. He's been dead, oh, 35 or 40 years.

From the beginning, Charlie had all the business he could handle. He'd farm in summer, work the winter in his shop. "It never rained, it never got cold, and Sundays never came lots of times," he says chuckling. "I just worked right on." Most of the work was repairing tools and farm equipment for his neighbors and farmers in the surrounding countryside. He'd shoe their horses and shrink their wagon wheels. The work hasn't changed much down through the years. He still shrinks a few wagon wheels every year, but he doesn't shoe horses anymore.

"I ain't shod a horse in 15 year. Last one I shod, I shod my own. Somebody stole my tools after that and I just quit. Way back yonder when I was shoeing horses, I'd furnish everything and put 'em on for 60¢." Even without the horseshoeing, there's still more work than Charlie can handle. "Just something to do continuously. They's never a blue day. Always something to do and I'm way behind. Folks'll come and I'll say, 'Well, I'll try to get to it. That's all I can tell you."

That's why there is no sign up by the road pointing out that Charlie's blacksmith shop is still doing business down the hill beyond the old house. Never has been a sign, never will be one.

"I don't want no more work," Charlie is saying. "I want to get away from work. Somebody's always drummin' for me. I told 'em somebody's goina get their butt kicked if they don't quit drummin' for me. I just can't do a day's work anymore. I'm wore out. I just can't stand it. I've been trying to quit for seven years. I've been trying to get some young man to take over and let me quit, but they won't do it . . . Hunh-uh . . . Too nasty. Well, the nasty won't kill you. If it would, I'da been gone a long time ago.

"I've tried my best to get some young man to come here and take it up. I tell 'em if he does good work and don't rob 'em, he can make a heap more money than he can at working public work. And he can be his own boss. They don't want it. Too much work to it. They's enough work here to keep four men working every day. These farmers, they just got to have it. Everybody says they ain't nobody blacksmithing anymore. It ain't no trouble to get welders, but they's so much of the stuff a welder can't do. Just continually somebody's coming in here wanting something different. Somebody's got a different idea every day, and I just go along with it. Don't bother me."

It's only because so many people need his services that Charlie puts in almost a full day in his shop every day. He can't let his neighbors and longtime customers down. If it weren't for that, he vows, he'd have quit already. But press him a little and he admits that quitting isn't really what he has in mind.

"Naw, I don't ever aim to *quit*. As long as I can get up and come down here, I want to come and work some, but I don't want to be *pushed*. I want to do a little something for myself, just make *me* some things."

August, 1976
Colfax, North Carolina

135

Fenderson Ballard
The Lord's Storekeeper

Everything is neat, painted blue and white, making Fenderson Ballard's house stand out among the shanties on the dead-end, rutted alley that is called Short Spring Street. To the people along Short Spring Street, Fenderson Ballard is known as "the reverend," and lots of times they laugh at him for beating his drum on Sunday morning. Reverend Ballard, as he prefers to be called, can tell his preaching isn't doing much good.

Bootleggers operate all around his little three-room house, and he can watch their customers coming and going, drinking rot-gut liquor and wasting their lives, helpless and hopeless. He prays for them but it goes right on.

People lie to Reverend Ballard when he asks them about coming to services and that makes him angry and he tells them off. "Don't y'all tell me 'bout you ain't got no stockin's. Just tell me you ain't comin' to church. Give God a fair deal."

Every Sunday morning, no matter the weather, Reverend Ballard removes the pink plaid blanket that covers his drum, carefully carries the drum outside and sets it up on his white picnic table. Then he begins to play it, chanting hymns with the beat. That's the call to services and sometimes somebody comes, but usually not.

That drum is Fenderson Ballard's joy. It's a fine drum, a big bass, and it cost him a lot of money. "I don't allow nobody to handle it but me," he said. "I beats it myself." He beats the drum and chants the hymns on Sunday mornings because he read in the Bible to "make a joyful noise unto the Lord." He couldn't think of any noise more joyful than the beat of a drum, but just any old drum wouldn't do. He bought the best drum he could find. "You got to have something good to glorify the Lord with . . ."

On a good Sunday, Reverend Ballard might have three or four show up for services. They sit on straight-back chairs in his front room. He plays spirituals on his record player, sometimes plays his guitar and sings hymns. And although he's 74 now, he springs to his feet, paces about, flails his arms and shouts. And when he gets wound up and really goes to preaching, those in attendance leave knowing they've been preached to. At those times Reverend Ballard gets so filled with joy that he cries.

"I didn't git no higher in school than third grade," he said. "Just barely can read and write. But I can read Scripture and I can get up and tell about it too."

Most of Fenderson Ballard's neighbors don't attend services. Those who do usually pass him by and go to the big church up the hill. Sometimes, though, children come, attracted by the drum, and Reverend Ballard holds Sunday School for them; then he preaches whether anybody has come to hear him or not.

It worries Reverend Ballard that so many of the people he sees around him seem so much more interested in receiving than giving. "They don't pay no tithes. No, they don't pay no tithes to the Lord." A dime out of every dollar Fenderson Ballard receives from Social Security goes to build up his "storehouse for the Lord."

The storehouse is in the room where he holds services. He has built shelves around the walls, and the shelves are stocked with corn flakes, coffee, soap, canned foods, baby food, brooms, stockings, all the things a little neighborhood store would have. Some of the stuff has been on the shelves for years. A picture of Jesus in a golden frame with a little light that doesn't work looks over the storehouse.

"I got a storehouse here like the Lord says," Reverend Ballard said. "That's what I got out of the Bible. Take your tithes and build up a storehouse for the Lord."

He never sells anything from the store, but he does give it away. When somebody is in need, he provides and prays. He often passes out pennies to the children who go to the big church up the hill so they can learn to tithe. Whenever there is sickness and no money for medicine, he gives that, too. "I want to help people. I don't rob. I don't take a nickel off them."

Sometimes those people who laugh at Reverend Ballard and lie to him and pass him by come and ask for help and they usually leave taking with them, at no charge, what they need from the shelves of his storehouse.

"That's the way I serve God," Fenderson Ballard said. "Jesus will pay me."

January, 1967
High Point, North Carolina

137

Wilbert Sullivan
The Rolling Grocery

The old truck, a '54 model, splotchy blue, creaks and rattles down the street and rumbles to a halt in a shady spot, always a shady spot.

A wooden top has been built over the back of the truck, and it sometimes moans under the crush of loaded soft drink crates that ride there. Boxes and bushel baskets filled with fresh vegetables bulge over the sides of the bed. A shelf in the middle is piled with soft bread, an insulated box packed with ice and cold drinks. Rows of Hershey bars, Sour Bits, Mary Janes, Sugar Mamas and other delights wait for eager little hands. A rusting hanging scale swings at the back. This is Wilbert Sullivan's Rolling Grocery, 37 years on the road.

The proprietor opens his door and slides halfway off his seat, resting a leg on the running board. Mr. Sullivan, they call him, or Buck, or Uncle Wilbert. He's a roly-poly man wearing OshKosh B'Gosh overalls and brogans. His blue eyes seem almost hidden in his round, smiling face, and his hair is growing white from the inside out.

If there are kids around, he has no need to announce his presence. They swarm from everywhere, yelling, "Hey, Mr. Sullivan." They hug him and climb over his truck. Overwrought mothers often tug and scold in vain attempts to keep them from squashing the tomatoes.

"I declare, Mr. Sullivan," says one mother, "you *are* a Pied Piper."

"This is *our* store," a child protests, and Wilbert Sullivan laughs.

In the cab of his truck, in a La Corona box, along with pencil stubs, receipts, notes and the Stanback pain-killing powders he frequently takes, he carries the school pictures they give him. Many are signed "With love . . ." in awkward scrawls.

When the kids are in school, Wilbert Sullivan just beeps his horn a couple of times and waits. His customers know his horn and emerge from their houses.

From Wilbert Sullivan's truck, customers can still get a half dozen fresh eggs in a brown paper bag, and the vegetables don't come coated with wax and wrapped in plastic. His customers

138

know, too, that if they're a little short, Mr. Sullivan will "put it on the book" and they can pay later. Equally important, they know they'll always get a smile and some chit-chat.

That's the way he's always operated. It was during the middle of the Depression that he came to Greensboro from a farm in Wayne County. He brought his wife, Myrtie, and his year-old daughter and the hope that he'd be able to find a job. Five days after his arrival, on November 14, 1931, his 22nd birthday, he got the job. It paid $5 a week. He went door-to-door selling produce off a truck, carrying his samples in two small baskets.

"I remember the first sale I made," he says. "Mr. and Mrs. Paul L. White. It was on Wednesday at 9 o'clock in the morning. I know the amount I sold them: 65¢ worth. In those days, if you sold 65¢ worth that was a load of stuff."

The Whites remained his customers when, a short time later, he went into business for himself; they are still his customers, as are many others. His routes are the same as they were 25 years ago. He sticks to the older residential sections, doesn't try to expand. He knows his customers and they know him and when to expect him. He knows all their family members and many of their ailments and problems.

"My customers is just like my own people," he says. "I love 'em to death. And I think they love me." That becomes evident as he makes his rounds. At one house he helps an elderly, invalid woman from her house. "She just loves to come out to my truck better than anything," he says later. At another stop, as a housewife picks among the vegetables, he says, "I used to hold her husband in my arms when he was a little baby. Now his children are buying from me.

"Them there's homegrown," he says to the woman, who is looking at a basket filled with fat pink tomatoes. "Them's the last I'll get I reckon."

Wilbert Sullivan's list of customers has been dwindling in recent years. "I've lost a lot that's passed away. Some's in old folks homes." At the same time he has had to cut back his work week. He had a heart attack a few years back and he has a blood circulation problem. Six months ago he hurt his leg and it still hasn't healed. It swells and he has to keep it bound. It's the middle of the day now before he starts his rounds, and he takes two days off each week instead of one, the way he used to do.

"I used to go all the time," he says, "but I can't now. I'm not able. All these years on these streets, it gets you down. But as long as I can walk around this truck I'm going to work. I don't sell a

139

Just Folks

whole lot, but I make a living."

September, 1968
Greensboro, North Carolina

Woodrow Allred
The Rooster's Friend

The sawmill had shut down for the day. All the other hands had gone, and Woodrow Allred was talking to his rooster. He nuzzled the rooster with his beard and said, "S'posed to go git you some scratch feed, ain't I? Huh? You like 'at scratch feed, don't you boy?"

It's gotten to the point Woodrow rarely talks to his rooster when the other hands are around. They make fun of him, especially when he talks baby talk, the way he usually does. They laugh when he insists the rooster talks to him, too.

"They say, 'You're crazy talkin' to anything like 'at'," he said indignantly. "Say, 'What you want to talk like 'at for?' Say, 'It's craziness.' " He gave a little snort and spat tobacco juice into the dirt. "They don't even know what you're talkin' about. This rooster does. You may not believe it, but this rooster's got plenty of sense. I git 'im up in my arms, talk to 'im. I say, 'Don't you love me? I love you.' He just goes *quonk-QUONK-quonk*, just like he's sayin' I love you."

He stroked the rooster's head. "Don't you?" The rooster softly quonk-quonk-quonked. Woodrow Allred grinned. "See there? You hear it?" He nuzzled the rooster again.

The rooster's name is Bill. Much of the time he is Woodrow's only companion, he and the fat hen Woodrow bought to keep Bill happy. The hen has no name. "That hen just as good to me as this rooster is, 'ough," he said. "I like both of 'em. I think there ain't nothin' like 'em."

Woodrow just turned 59. He has been a sawmill worker for 29 of those years. Five days a week, from 7:30 a.m. until 3:30 p.m., he takes lumber off the conveyor as it comes from the saw. But unlike the other hands who go home at the end of the work day, he remains at the mill. "I watch after this mill. Anybody comes messin' aroun', ol' Bill lets me know. He tells me ever' time anybody's comin'. If there's anybody comin', he'll go to crowin'.''

Woodrow Allred's home is a shack built of rough lumber and sheet metal, mounted on wheels so it can be moved with the sawmill from wooded site to wooded site. He has few conveniences: a small wood stove for heating and cooking, a pile of grimy mattresses amidst the clutter for a bed. There is no bathroom, no running water, no electricity. He moved into the shack and started staying with the sawmill eight years ago after his wife, Lizzie, died. The only time he leaves is for a couple of hours to buy groceries on Friday afternoons.

"I was married 14 years," he said. "I been without a woman eight year. My wife died eight year ago. I miss 'er. Boy, don't I 'ough . . . Ain't nobody but myself and these chickens, but they's one thing about it, we enjoy ourselves. Don't we?" he said to Bill.

He's had the chickens only eight months. "See, I had a dog to start with. Ol' Spotty. I loved ol' Spotty. I had the dog five year and he got stole from me. Ol' Spotty was really good. I hated he got gone. After Ol' Spotty got gone, I got me a pig when we was over yonder other side of Staley, and he got stole too. I got 'im to eat, but I make a pet of everything I git. I give 60 dollars for 'at hog. Three days after I got 'im paid for somebody come in there and toted 'im off. So I got me these chickens."

It wasn't long after he got the chickens that he came to believe the rooster was trying to talk to him. "When I got 'em, I didn't know nothin' to talk to 'em about. I'd go get 'em out of the box, rub 'em, talk to 'em. One day I was gittin' 'at rooster out and I seen they didn't have no water. I said, 'Are you out of water?' He said *quonk-quonk-quonkquonk*. Sounded just like he said, 'Out of water.' He's been talkin' like 'at ever since.

"The funniest part about it, see, I got a chainsaw here, little ol' bitty chainsaw. I'as over 'ere cuttin' some wood with it one day. Bill, he can't stand a chainsaw. I'as cuttin' and it quit. Wouldn't start back. I said, 'Dadburn you! I ought to pick up that derned ax and chop you into little bitty pieces.' I tried it ag'in and it still wouldn't start. I started back up here and I heard ol' Bill. He said, 'I'm sure glad it didn't start.' I said, 'Shut up, Bill, or I'll come up 'ere and beat your tail.' He said it ag'in, just crowed. Made me mad. He don't like a chainsaw. Now 'at hen don't pay no 'tention to nothin'."

He put Bill back in his coop, cooing to him, then sat in the doorway of his shack. "I know they goina git stole from me, or a snake'll git 'em, or sumpin," he said. "But I sure do like havin' 'em around. I like to have a little ol' pet. I did have a pet here in the house but I got shet of that job. He got where he eat more'n I did. Little ol' mouse. Eat my loafbread. I like my loafbread, my loafbread and my beans. White beans. Boy, give me a pot of 'em white beans. I love 'em things. But I don't like pintos. I don't eat them pintos . . .

142

"Yeah, ol' bachelor sees a hard time. I been cookin' my own rations since my wife died. I had a good woman. She is dead and gone, but I had a good'un. I wouldn't taken a share in a gold mine for 'at woman. The Good Man knowed the best, I reckon. He knowed all about 'er. He made 'er heart quit beatin'. He's goina make mine quit hurtin' one of 'ese days. . . ."

For a few moments he sat saying nothing, looking up the hill toward the mill, where the big saw sat silent. "What I want to do, I want to be at the sawmill when the Good Man calls me. Yessir, I love the sawmill, and I'm goina stay right here till the Good Man comes and takes me away."

July, 1977
Cedar Falls, North Carolina

Lee Goldston
Log Snaker

I could hear him singing in the woods high on the side of the little mountain, his voice growing louder as I climbed. It was a rich voice, deep and melodic and mournful, rising and falling. During his pauses I could hear the crashing in the trees.

Up there somewhere, I knew, Lee Goldston was at work, he and Sandy, his brawny, ton-heavy Belgian horse. Sandy is one of two Belgians Lee Goldston works. The other, Big Boy, is a couple of hundred pounds lighter. Lee Goldston has had the horses for almost seven years and anybody else probably would have a difficult time working them.

Sandy and Big Boy do not respond to "gee" and "haw" and other such ordinary conversation between man and horse. They respond only to Lee Goldston's singing.

"Yeh-ehhhhh-ehhh-ahhhh . . . Lawd, Lawd, Lawd . . . I can't he'p I'm cryin' . . . Whoa-ohhh-ohhh-oh . . ."

He stopped work when he saw me, pushed back his hat and wiped his forehead. He was wearing overalls and chewing a blackgum twig, a "toothbrush," he calls it. He grinned when I asked about his horses.

"Trained 'em myself," he said. "You don't have to talk to 'em like you do other horses. That's the way I trained 'em. I started out singin' to 'em. Git 'em right took me about six months. I've broke a many a one in my life. All I train, I sing to 'em."

Lee Goldston's work is snaking logs. Loggers cut the trees, top and section them. Lee and his horses drag the logs from the woods and stack them for the sawmill tractors to pick up. He is 54 and he has been at this work since he was 13, although he has done farm work too. "I'd ruther do this than anything I ever done," he said. "Don't many people snake logs. Now the old people do. These young people don't know much about it."

Like everything else, the job of snaking logs from the woods has become mechanized, but Lee Goldston has never used anything but horses and mules. He works for himself, hiring out his services to sawmill operators. In addition to his horses, he owns three tractors equipped for hauling big stacks of logs to the mill. He lets his hired hands drive the tractors. He can always be found in the woods, snaking and stacking logs with his horses for the men on the tractors to haul away.

Until he got Sandy and Big Boy, Lee Goldston used mules for the job. But after he saw one of those big Belgians at work on a farm, he decided he had to have some of his own. The horses are very special to him, and he loves to show people how they work, responding to his singing.

"They know just as good what I'm singin'. You won't know, but they do. I just got different words they know . . . I want to show you somethin'. You watch 'im now. He knows what I say, but you won't."

He went off up the hill singing to Sandy and the two of them started hauling logs down and lining them up. A second row was put atop the first, the big horse climbing onto the first row, balancing carefully on the big logs as he pulled and pushed the second row into place. The third row was the tricky one. Lee Goldston talked Sandy through it.

"Come on Son, he'p Daddy, he'p me a little more Sugar. Back Son. He'p me little bit, Sugar. He'p Daddy, Son. Touch it. Touch it light. That's a good hoss."

The logs fell right into place. Lee Goldston grinned proudly. "You ever see one like it? Don't he know how to log? He knows exactly what you say, don't he?" I had to agree. It was a thing of sheer beauty, perfect coordination between man and horse and I told him so.

"Money won't buy 'im," Lee Goldston said. "I wouldn't take nothin' for either one of 'em. I think about as much of one as I do the other. I been offered a thousand dollars for Sandy. I carried 'im to the pullin' contest. He outpulled everything up there. I took 'im to Reidsville. Yeah, he's the champ. He lacked 400 pound pullin' as much as any two horses up there. You wouldn't sell 'im either, would you?"

It was a long way back down the mountain, but for much of the way I still could hear them up there working, and even beyond that I still could hear Lee Goldston singing.

"It's all-l-l-l right. It's all ri-i-i-i-ght. Yeh-ehhhhhhh-ehhhhh-eh . . ."

August, 1977
Asheboro, North Carolina

145

A Turnabout's Fair Play

It is set back from the road a ways, beyond the big oak tree. Not a big building. It's fashioned of corrugated metal, and it looks as if it is about to fall down. Old furniture is propped against the walls. Over the door, a sign painted by the Coca-Cola people says, "We Buy, Sell Or Trade For Anything. Auction Sale 7:30 Sat. Night."

Inside, the dirt floor is littered with cigarette butts. The walls are papered with flattened cardboard boxes. There are several rows of benches covered with cardboard, two old church pews and a couple of dirty sofas with the stuffing sprouting.

Several men sit warming themselves around a metal drum with a stovepipe leading out the top and through the roof. "I had this thing goin' good," says the big man, the one called Red. "Since I been sick, it kindly fell a little bit from what it was."

The place is called Red's Auction House. A crudely painted sign tacked to a rafter advises that the house gets 15 per cent of all sales and that Red can't be responsible for fire, theft or natural calamity. "Warning," says another sign on a wall, "All intoxication, curse'n, or filthy language are forbidden. Any one breaking these rules will be prosecuted by law."

Some Saturday nights at Red's have seen crowds of as many as 200 people. They come toting whatever they've got to sell. "Anything," says Red. "Odd and end stuff. People brings it in automobiles, trucks, cars. What they don't sell they take back. Sell anything you bring — 10¢ to five dollars. They sold some televisions down here Saturday night for a dollar a piece. One of 'em played."

Red's was closed for a while recently, and the sales are just getting started again. Red was sick. The high blood, as he calls it, hit him back before Christmas. "I didn't know I was in the world Christmas," he says. He lost more than 100 pounds during his sickness, but he's still a big man. "I'as right at 300 'fore I got sick," he says.

It was Red's eyes that put him in the auction and trading business more than 30 years ago. His first job was in a furniture factory. Then he set himself up in the trucking business, hauling sand, watermelons, anything that needed hauling. "I'as driving a truck the first time I ever knowed my eyes was going to the bad. See a car coming of a night, look like they was two." He is now blind in one eye and can barely see with the other. He started trading and auctioning because it was something he could do. "I don't say I like it, but that's about the only way I got of making anything. Don't make much at that in the wintertime. Now, in the summertime, you make purty good. See, I don't draw nothin'."

Through the years, Red figures he's sold a little of almost everything. "I've traded mules, traded goats, buy, sell, trade ducks, chickens, dogs. I've even sold snakes, copperhead, blacksnake, king snake . . . I ain't been into no fraish deals right lately on account of bein' sick. Ain't been in none since last summer." In all those years of trading, Red says he's only been taken once. "I'as down in the bed two years, I mean *in* the bed, and an old man come here, he found out the doctors wanted me to have a milk goat to drink milk from." The man sold Red a goat for $15, said it would give half a gallon a day. "Why, we didn't get half a pint," Red said. His wife wanted him to take the goat back but Red said no. "If I ever get out of the bed," he said, "I'll get even with him."

Red finally did get out of the bed, and one day he took a flock of little White Leghorn roosters he'd raised and traded them for a big nanny that looked as if she'd give gallons of milk daily. The goat, in fact, was almost dry and that was precisely what Red wanted. One day he saw the old man who had traded him the goat when he was sick coming down the road with his mule. "I went and got me a big can of condensed milk," Red said, "stobbed a hole in it and poured the milk in a milk bucket . . . He come up down there, walked up behind me. I was settin' there with both hands like I was milkin.' He says, 'That goat sure pours it, don't she?' I said, 'Yeah, it does.' He stood there a minute or two and said, 'I'd like to have that goat.' I said, 'Well, I bought it to keep, but I reckon you could get it.' "

They settled on $18.50, and the old man led the goat home. "He come back a day or two after that, said to me, says, 'I know damn well that old goat give milk, I seen you milkin' it, she won't do it now.' 'Well, I don't know about that,' I said."

The old man told Red his wife figured goats were like cows, move them around they get upset and won't give, and Red allowed how that was probably true. Later, some fellows who knew Red told the old man what Red had done and kidded him about it, and the old man came back hopping mad. "Got so mad he'as about to fight. I just admitted ever'thing and he just stood there. I says, 'You know what, Ed? A turnabout's a fair play."

March, 1969
Thomasville, North Carolina

Cliff Taylor
Rattlesnake Man

At one time, there were 24 rattlesnakes, four copperheads and a big cottonmouth in the wood and glass cage out beside the store. "When we had the window up, you could hear 'em singing in here," Cliff Taylor said.

People used to come from all around to see Cliff Taylor's snakes and hear his tales. On summer weekends, the parking lot of the little store and bait shop he runs on Highway 8, near Tuckertown Lake, would be filled with cars.

"My friends and myself, in years past, caught 50, 60, 70 a year," he said. He was sitting in a straight-back chair in his store. He is a big man, red-faced, with thinning hair. He is laconic and slow-talking when he does speak. "Not many last year. About a dozen. Year before about 25 or 30."

All of those snakes were caught within a few miles of the store, the rear of which doubles as Cliff Taylor's home. The store sits smack in the middle of the Uwharrie Mountains, that ancient and well-worn range in the south-central part of North Carolina. The Uwharries, Cliff Taylor is quick to tell you, are "pure ol' snake country."

But this year, for the first time in many years, the Uwharrie rattlers (there are two kinds, canebrake and timber) may not have to contend with Cliff Taylor sniffing around. That's what he does, he will tell you: sniff them out. He claims he can smell a rattlesnake from as far as 50 feet away. "It's kindly a rotten scent to it . . ." he said. "You take a blacksnake and a copperhead smell a whole lot like a rotten cucumber. A rattler . . ." he grinned ". . . it's like a baby diaper that's got old. It's a purty bad odor."

Cliff says he learned to smell out snakes and capture them as a young man when he went to work as a section hand on the South-bound Railroad that passes through the Uwharries. Rattlesnakes liked to sun themselves on the railroad bed. "That place was loaded up and down with 'em." He and the other workers would tie their boot strings into loops on long sticks and use them to catch snakes. He doesn't remember exactly why they did it. "Just catchin' 'em, seein' if we could, I reckon. Most people said it was a lackin' of sense."

Whatever the reason, Cliff enjoyed it and kept at it through the years. He always kept a snake stick and covered bucket in his car, just in case. Sometimes he would happen onto snakes as they crossed roads. Sometimes a neighbor would come upon a rattler in the garden and call Cliff to come and get it. Sometimes he and his friends would just go out and hunt them around slab piles and rocks. It was a tricky business, of course, but Cliff was never bitten, although he had some close calls.

"I've had 'em loose up in my arms," he said. "They just missed me, that's all."

He never harmed the snakes. He would keep them at the store for people to look at and then he'd give them away or sell them. He gave some to museums and zoos. Most he sold to a fellow from Wilmington who distributed them to zoos, serpentariums, educational institutions. The going rate was a dollar a foot. It was never a profitable thing for Cliff Taylor — he made much more trapping snapping turtles in Tuckertown Lake — but money wasn't why he did it.

"I tell you, it's a big thrill to catch a rattlesnake," he said. "Same as killin' a big buck deer. Makes your blood pressure go up. Doctor told me to leave 'em alone."

High blood pressure hit Cliff in recent months, and his doctor ordered him to take it easy and give up snake hunting. That won't be easy for Cliff.

"Oh, I'm liable to have some snakes sometime," he said. "I might patch up the old cage. I won't go *huntin'* 'em now, but if somebody tells me where one's at, I'll come pick it up for 'em. I might catch a big rattlesnake crossing the road sometime. They cross number eight here a lot . . ."

May, 1975
Jackson Hill, North Carolina

149

Peg Leg Jackson
The Last Medicine Show

The afternoon heat was heavy in the room, oppressive like the heat of July or August. Almost no air stirred. The window was closed, still covered outside with the clear plastic that had kept out the winter winds. A fat wasp took flight from a corner of a windowpane and buzzed lazily over the bed where the old man lay.

The old man had a dark, lean face with a vicious scar across the right side. "Twelve-gauge shotgun done that," he said later, offering no further explanation. The scar had claimed half his ear. His hair, what was left of it, lay in tiny gray coils on his head, and his gray goatee seemed to stand on his chin. Even in the heat his body was under the covers. The wooden leg was propped against the foot of the bed.

Peg Leg Jackson hadn't been up all day. The miseries were upon him, had been for several days. There had been considerable debate about just what had brought on this attack. John Glenn's wife maintained it was those green beans, so heavy with grease, that he had eaten the other night. But in Peg Leg's mind the matter was settled.

"Eat too much po'k," he said. "High blood, you know . . . I love hog meat, you see. Appetite's goin' be the death of me, I reckon."

Another white boy had come. He sat by the bed fiddling with a tape recorder that wouldn't work. In recent years, there had been a lot of eager white faces, mostly young, drawn to Peg Leg's side. He always made time for them, even when he had the miseries. They often had tape recorders, and they wanted him to tell his lies into them, sing his songs and play his mouth harp. Some had been almost reverent, convinced, it seemed, that locked somewhere inside Peg Leg's harmonica were the very secrets of life.

It was true Peg Leg need only play his mouth harp and all of life's miseries and joys would come tumbling out. He could make that thing talk and laugh and cry. And if those who had come were lucky and got him liquored up enough, got him *right*, Peg Leg might even dance. Yes, dance, with that peg leg flying, that leg he carved himself kicking high.

"Shoot, he can dance better'n he can play them harps," Peg

Leg's friend, John Glenn, said. "Oh Lord, you should see him dance. He can put on a show, I tell you that."

Once, a few years back, some white folks had come from New York to see Peg Leg. They had brought sophisticated recording equipment and plenty of liquor and that night Peg Leg had got right, he and Baby Tate. The result was playing loud now on John Glenn's record player. And for the first time all day, Peg Leg began to stir, responding to the music.

". . . Ain't but one thing, buddy boy, give a man the blues . . ." his voice was singing from the other room.

"Yes, Lord," he said, nodding to the music.

A guitar boogie came on with Peg Leg playing harmonica accompaniment, and he tried to snap his fingers. "That ol' Baby Tate. Yeah, Baby Tate Boogie. He stayed in Greenville. Ol' Baby Tate pump 'at thing, don't he boy? He's dead now. Yeah, Lord, that the first record I made. Full of whiskey. Good corn likker . . . I had my likker settin' in 'tween my legs when I was makin' 'at record. I made 'at record in Spa't'nburg. Right out there behind the Co-Cola plant, John. Spa't'nburg."

Peg Leg had been at John Glenn's house for about two weeks this time. Through the years, he had known he always had a place at John Glenn's. They had been raised together, dirt-poor, in the country near Jonesville. Glenn settled down close to home, but he knew his friend (he calls him Ol' Peg and seems to chuckle every time he says the name) was born to roam.

Arthur Jackson was 10 when he first ran away from home. "First time I run away, I stayed three weeks. Next time, I stayed away, I think about four months. I kept stayin' longer, goin' a little farther all the time . . . I didn't know what I was goin' do. I was doin' some of anything. I wanted to be anything."

He learned to ride the freight trains, and he was riding one in Raleigh when he lost his leg. "I was just down from Cincinnati when I got my leg off. I believe I was asleep. All I know, when I woke up, part of my body was gone." He recuperated at home. An old man made him a peg leg, and when he started to learn to walk on it, his mama began to worry that he would take off again. John Glenn drew the task of seeing that he didn't. An impossible job, he discovered. One day in the woods Peg Leg slipped away from him and was gone. Glenn recalls going back to report, "Peg done run ag'in."

After that, nobody ever knew when to expect him around Jonesville. It might be two years, or it might be eight. He always came back, but he always was just passing through. "Drifter," he

151

said, "just a drifter."

He learned to play the harmonica when he was eight or nine, and he hooked up with a medicine show man. "I drawed a crowd for 'im, you see. We had a little stage like. I'd put on an exhibition for 'im. I played a harmonica, then tell lies. I'm the biggest liar you ever seen. When the crowds got heavy enough, then he'd talk and I'd pass it out. He have three or four different items, you know, snake oil, tonic . . ."

Arthur Jackson started calling himself Peg Leg Sam. He considered himself a showman. In the late summer and fall he worked the tobacco warehouses. In the colder months he hoboed about the country playing in joints and on the streets. "I wear out a harp a day when I was buskin'. You don't know what buskin' is, do you? Buskin' passin' the hat aroun' for nickles, dimes and quarters."

His health stayed good . . . "All but when I'd git in a knife fight. Great God a'mighty." And somehow he always got by, always kept moving. "Yeah, I been over the United States a hundred times." Always, too, he went back to the medicine shows. In the early '30s, he met a medicine show man in Smithfield, North Carolina, who called himself Chief Thundercloud, an Indian from Oklahoma. Off and on, they worked with each other for nearly 40 years.

"Sometimes I wouldn't see Chief for a year, two years, but he'd come back and git me." Right up until a few years ago, Peg Leg and the chief would hit the road in the springtime, just as they always had, and work the country towns in the Midwest and Deep South. Peg Leg believes they were the only medicine show still going. "Last. We was the last one. Me and Chief. Ol' Chief died about three years ago."

"The Last Medicine Show" was the name of Peg Leg Sam's first record album, the one that he and his friend, Baby Tate, made while they were drunk in Spartanburg that night. It was still playing on John Glenn's record player. Songs such as "Skinny Woman Blues," "Peg Leg's Fox Run," "Greasy Greens." Peg Leg lay on the bed listening.

"I just had a second grade reader," he said, as if talking to himself. "Wonder how I could make up all them songs?"

The wonder is that it took the young people and folklorists so long to discover Peg Leg Sam. That happened only six or seven years ago. Peg Leg can't remember exactly. They started coming to him wanting him to play at "folk festivals." He always was happy to go. First thing he knew, he had a record album and a booking agent in New York. "I played Chicago," he said, "Philadelphia, a big one. El Paso, Texas. All them. Washington, D.C., New York City. See, they pay my way up there and back. Pay for all my eatin', all my sleepin'. Don't cost me nothin'."

Four more record albums followed that first one (Did Peg Leg make any money on them? "So much it leak right out my pocket."), and he cut another one back in the winter when he was passing through New York on his way home from Canada. Since then, he hasn't been anywhere, sticking close to the shanty he shares with his brother a few miles out of Jonesville, or putting up at John Glenn's. He's been turning down appearances, he says, and for the first time in his life, he hasn't felt like moving on . . .

"Done run out," he said. "I give up, might near. Too old. Good God. Half sickly too. Devil gittin' to me now for the deeds I done, I reckon. But I ain't never hurt nobody. Naw suh. *My* lies ain't like them other lies I tell, you know."

The white boy had one last question. "If you could live your life over, would you do it differently?"

Peg Leg looked at him for a long time saying nothing, as if the question were not worthy of an answer. "Yeah," he said finally, "I'd start earlier."

June, 1977
Whitestone, South Carolina

Peg Leg Jackson got to feeling better after I visited him, and in the summer of 1977 went to Canada to make another appearance at a folk music festival. It was his last. He fell ill again after returning home and died in September. He is buried in a small church cemetery not far from the shanty he called home.

The Mountains

ZSCHIESCHE

Clara Edwards
Mistress of Oak Hall

On a misty afternoon, it appears as a ghostly presence hovering on the hillside overlooking the town.

Oak Hall, it is called. For nearly 100 years, it has been Tryon's dominant landmark, once the winter refuge of the rich and famous.

Lady Nancy Astor used to come with her entourage. Thomas Edison, Henry Ford, Mrs. Calvin Coolidge all stayed here. So did David Niven. F. Scott Fitzgerald spent a winter and spring at Oak Hall. General George Marshall's widow lived more than 10 years in a downstairs room.

Now the elegance is frayed. Paint is peeling. Kudzu twines through the grounds. Creaky, rambling Oak Hall is in its last days as a hotel.

"Do you want to see Scott Fitzgerald's room?" Clara Edwards asks.

We climb the stairs to the wide, high-ceilinged hallway on the third floor. "This is the same rug he walked on," she says.

His was a corner room. It has changed little since he occupied it. The bed with the huge walnut headboard is the same one in which he slept.

"The best thing about it is the view," Clara says. She points out Tryon Peak, White Oak Peak, Big and Little Warrior Mountains in the distance. "Misseldine's Drug Store was right in front of that little yellow car down there," she says, pointing over the tree tops to Main Street below, "and the post office was right over there."

The year was 1937. Scott Fitzgerald had come to Oak Hall at the suggestion of friends to fight his alcoholism and mild tuberculosis. He was troubled by the insanity of his wife, Zelda, who was in a private sanitarium in nearby Asheville. Here, he hoped to recapture his failing talent as a writer.

Clara Edwards was 30 then, unmarried (as she would remain), working as assistant postmistress. Each morning, she set aside Fitzgerald's mail; when he came for it, he would invite her to Misseldine's, where he often gathered with friends for a cup of coffee or a soda. One morning he scribbled a bit of doggerel about the drug store on a paper napkin and handed it to her ("Oh Misseldine's, dear Misseldine's/A dive we'll ne'er forget/The taste of its banana splits/Is on our tonsils yet"). She smiles at the memory.

Clara Edwards had always loved Oak Hall. She often attended social functions at the hotel, never thinking she would own it one day. But in 1948, when it came up for sale, she got a loan from the bank and bought it.

"It's been the dream of my life, I tell you that," she says. "It was hard to pay for, but I paid for it."

She moved in, opened the hotel year-round and went to work day and night, rarely taking vacations. Under her direction, the dining room became famous for its food, particularly its cheese soufflé and spoonbread, as well as for the service provided by its waiters, two of whom, Ted King and Nonie Robinson, have worked at the hotel for more than 40 years.

Clara Edwards sits now at a dining room table and sighs. "I had a group of teachers last night from Columbia and Spartanburg, said they just had to come one more time, and I fed them chess pie and homemade bread about midnight and left them playing bridge."

Several weeks earlier, shortly after the death of her brother, Frank, who had tended grounds at Oak Hall, Clara Edwards had sold the hotel.

"I wasn't thinking about selling, to tell you the truth," she says. "My doctors were doing my thinking. They advised me to sell it years ago, but I just wouldn't listen."

Her plans, she says, are to close the 66-room hotel soon after the fall leaf season and vacate it shortly thereafter. She sold it to two Virginia brothers, who have told her they plan to tear it down and build condominiums.

"I felt like I was giving my life away, if you want to know the truth," she says of the sale. "It really has torn up a lot of people. It's sad for me. I've shed enough tears to float an army. After you've been in something so long and love it and . . . well . . . it's a wonderful spot, a wonderful old landmark that's passing away."

I ask what she will do after she has closed it.

"Oh, I'll have someplace here in Tryon, but I'm not sure yet."

"Are you going to just take it easy?"

"I hope so. But I won't ever be as happy doing that as I have been right here."

August, 1979
Tryon, North Carolina

Just Folks

Della Shehan, Oak Hall's longtime housekeeper, watched silently from the staircase, barricaded by plywood and "No Admittance" signs, as crowds milled through the hallway below, poking and examining.

The rooms Della Shehan had cleaned so many times were empty now, the furnishings tagged and piled in the downstairs hallway, the parlor, lobby and club meeting room.

It had been two weeks since the hotel's rooms last held guests, since the last meal had been served in the elegant dining room. Now the dining room was jammed with people waiting for the auction to begin.

"I hate to see it," Della Shehan said, shaking her head. "I don't guess I'll look for other work. I'm getting old and I guess I ought to quit. Anyway, I couldn't never find another Clara Edwards to work for. She's awful upset."

Clara Edwards was not at the hotel for the auction. The night before, quite ill and crying, she was taken from her room to the home of a niece, Marty Copenhaver. Earlier this morning, she had tried to get out of bed and had fallen, fracturing several ribs and cutting her head. As the auction of her hotel's furnishings was about to begin, she was being admitted to St. Luke's Hospital in nearby Columbus.

Ted King and Nonie Robinson stood in the kitchen door watching as crowds filled the dining room where they had waited tables for so many years. The crowd overflowed into the lobby and onto the wide porch. In the kitchen, strangers, employees of a catering company, were preparing soggy barbecue sandwiches and hot dogs to be sold to the crowd.

"I see'd a lot of things happen here," Nonie Robinson said, "but I never thought I'd see this. How I feel about it? Just like you lost your best friend, that's how."

The first items offered for sale by the auctioneer, two chipped, painted wooden candlesticks, were sold for $10 to a local real estate agent who said he was buying them for some Michigan neighbors of Henry Ford who had been coming to Oak Hall for 40 years.

The prices bid for some of the most unremarkable items were remarkably high, so high that some of the antique dealers who had gathered from several states in hopes of picking up bargains soon left.

"Sentiment!" one of them said, almost spitting the word. "They're buying for sentiment. You can't eat sentiment."

Catherine Stephenson of nearby Bat Cave was one buyer who

admitted her sentiment. She was moved to tears when her $75 bid won a cheap recliner with its vinyl upholstery torn and taped. The chair had been a favorite of Katherine Marshall, widow of General George C. Marshall, in the years she lived at the hotel before her death.

Catherine Stephenson's husband, Bill, a high official in the Roosevelt administration and later a Harvard dean, was a member of General Marshall's staff during the early stages of World War II. They became close friends, and so did their wives.

"You know what she used to say about this place?" Catherine Stephenson asked. "She called this a first-rate second-class hotel."

It wasn't until the second day of the auction that the walnut bed and marble-topped dresser from Scott Fitzgerald's room were sold. Bill and Carol Wiggins of Gaffney, South Carolina, bought them for $1,250. The big, ornate, hand-carved walnut bar from the dining room went for $8,000 to Roscoe Green of Tuxedo, who said he planned to use it for a drawing card in a gift shop.

The planned two-day sale stretched to three. By the end of the third day, almost everything was gone. The following morning, workers for the auction company were stacking folding chairs in the dining room. Della Shehan busied herself taking down curtains. Nonie Robinson and Ted King helped clean up the mess left by the crowds.

"It's not business as usual, it's business as unusual," said Marty Copenhaver, "but everybody's here. We're organizing what's left."

Clara Edwards was reported to be resting comfortably under sedation at the hospital. "She's in pretty good spirits," said her niece. "She'll be all right. She's a brave little gal. This is so hard on her, but she bounces back. Everybody is standing stalwart behind her."

November, 1979
Tryon, North Carolina

George Owl
Indian Boyhood

It was a beautiful fall afternoon. George Owl sat on the porch of his refurbished log cabin, a cabin his father and grandfather had built in a nook of Rattlesnake Mountain many years earlier.

"Listen to the quiet," he said. "Hear how quiet it is?"

There was only the sound of the wind swaying the trees and the crackling of dry leaves as they fluttered on the wind and scudded across the porch.

"This is the most peaceful place in the world as far as I'm concerned," he said.

At 75, George Owl is a distinguished looking man with white hair and a face that looks cast in bronze. His blood is three-fourths Cherokee. He was born on the reservation, went away to school in Virginia, and became the first Cherokee drafted in World War I. After the war, he played professional baseball before ending up in New England, where he lived until World War II, when he rejoined the Army at age 47. After his second war, he returned to Cherokee.

"It's the only home I'll ever think of as home," he said.

He served a term as chairman of the Tribal Council and rebuilt his father's old log house, hauling the materials up the mountain trail with a mule and sled. "We lived like the old mountaineers," he recalled. "No lights. Cooked by the fireplace."

There are lights now, an electric cookstove, a road that George Owl built up the mountain. He and his wife, a former professor at the University of Oklahoma, are retired now. They live in Cherokee from early spring until mid-fall, the best time to be in the mountains, and then they go west to Oklahoma.

On this afternoon, Isaac Davis, a wiry, springy little man of 70, a retired construction worker who lives down the mountain, had walked up for a visit. He sat, leaning on a walking stick. It was a time for reminiscing. George Owl was doing most of the talking. Isaac Davis would nod approval, erupting now and then in nostalgic laughter.

George Owl was talking about his boyhood on the reservation, about how he was taken from home at age six and put in the government's boarding school and not allowed to visit home but once a month, even though home was just up the mountain. "You had a lot of Indian boys wouldn't stay in school," he said. "They'd run, go home. They got so they would punish us . . . The ones who ran were chained to the bedstead at night. Now, that's the truth. With chains . . . They finally had a dungeon, a jail with bars on it. Isn't that right?"

"That's the truth," said Isaac Davis, chuckling at the memory.

"They had a couple of fellows in the jail one night," George Owl went on, "that dungeon, they found a hole knocked in the wall next morning, the kids were gone . . ."

The two culprits were promptly captured, returned to the dungeon, chained to their beds this time, he said, laughing. ". . . The next morning when they went to check on them, they found the bedstead and all was gone. They found the bedstead out here in the woods, the chain beaten off with a rock . . ."

Isaac Davis joined in the laughter.

"My uncle was bad to run away," George Owl said. "He's a preacher now."

He then recalled how he was whipped and had his mouth washed out with soap for speaking the Cherokee language. "Oh, I'm telling you, that was a mess. I remember those days. But we had a lot of fun, too. We played Indian stick ball, billy-billy-bee, shinny. I remember my first experience with shinny . . ."

Shinny was a game like ice hockey, played on a field with clubs and a ball made from the burned knot of a chestnut tree. ". . . That ball caught me on the chin. I still have the scar. And I played stick ball, I *played* that. I mean the *old, old* way . . ."

By that, George Owl meant he played when the game was taken seriously, when every Indian community had a team and every game resulted in players being nearly choked to death, leaving with bloodied heads and broken limbs. Football without rules. George Owl was launched now into a description of his initiation as a stickball player. It was a ritual during which the medicine man put long scratches all over his body with a bird claw ("bled just like a hog"), then swabbed the cuts with a turpentine-like solution made from pine needles. This was followed by a festival with dancing all night, then a forced march, sometimes as far as 12 miles through the roughest unmarked country so that rival medicine men couldn't anticipate the route and scatter bad luck herbs in their path. The battle itself, the game, would take place on freshly mown hay field studded with briars.

George Owl shook his head. Isaac Davis grinned.

Just Folks

"How in the world a person played a game like that and enjoyed it, I don't know," George Owl said. "But it was a real enjoyable game. I think it was one of the best things for building a person up for hardship and obedience. I tell you, once I got that ball, I was gone. He can tell you that." He nodded at Isaac Davis.

"He *was* that," Davis said, chuckling.

"Yes sir," George Owl said. "I got that ball and *I* was gone. Nobody could touch me. I scored nine goals in one game."

November, 1970
Cherokee, North Carolina

Stafford Hartley
Mountain Columnist

While the breezes whine
Through the tall, tall pines
And the love strings
Around your heart entwine,
May your star above shine brighter,
And your load of cares grow lighter,
As your old man of the mountains
Fades away . . .

Stafford Hartley

The road, if it could be called that, clings to the mountainside, rising, dipping, twining, barely wide enough for one vehicle, muddy and so deeply rutted that the driver of a small car might reasonably fear turning over should a wheel be allowed to slip.

At the end of the road, where the view opens magnificently, a small brick house perches on the mountainside, the house Stafford Hartley built for himself after his wood house burned more than 25 years ago.

"I been in most of the winter," he says. "Oh God, yeah, it's been awful. Really been rough. *Really* been rough. In other words, we have had anywhere from six to eleven inches of solid ice on this road."

It has been a rough winter in other ways, too. A bad heart and other infirmities of his 75 years have taken their toll on Stafford Hartley. He settles into a straight-back chair by the fireplace in the main room of his house, stoking the fire to knock the late afternoon chill off the room. "I just about lost a winter's work. 'Bout lost this one."

Only 16 shiny dulcimers hang on the wall, less than half his normal winter's output. "I started in September and that's what I got."

Dulcimer making is just one of Stafford Hartley's talents. He is better known as philosopher, humorist, public speaker, newspaper columnist, and general, all-around cantankerous character. "I'm nothin' more than just what you're lookin' at," he

163

says, "a poor, uneducated old mountain man who loves nice people. I've never owned a suit of clothes in my life. Wherever I go, I go dressed in overalls and a overall jacket."

He has been a lot of places. He's traveled 15 states at one time or another, even dipped down into Mexico once. In recent years, he was in demand as a public speaker and he was regularly going off to Charlotte, or Winston-Salem, or some other place to talk. "I don't mean to go into it, but I think I'm a purty good poet. I'm a purty good comedian. I've never been booed and shouted down and egg-splattered." But that is past. "My doctor told me to quit that or I'd be down under in six months. It's hard to do. Oh, God, fella, it dern near killed me to have to give up my speechmaking. But I'm just not able to do it anymore."

Even harder was giving up his column. Through the years, Stafford Hartley, calling himself the self-elected mayor of Bailey's Camp, has written columns for several mountain newspapers. By last May, when he decided to quit after a spell of serious illness, he was writing for only one paper, the *Granite Falls Press*. "There was my farewell column," he says, after searching through a stack of old papers for it. The column worked. Letters poured in begging him not to quit. "And I had to come back," he says with a shrug. But he missed a few columns during the winter, and writing gets harder all the time.

"Sometime a little column like that, I work three or four days on it, maybe 15 minutes at a time. In other words, my hand cramps. But I can't quit as long as I can use that hand at all."

When he gets fired up, Stafford Hartley can still churn one out. And he still gets fired up, no question about that. He is fired up because the newspaper at Blowing Rock, the *Rocket*, dropped his column five years ago. "I can get mean as hell, fella," he says. "The only way I'll ever write for that *Rocket* again is for them to give me a front page apology and for them to run a picture of this danged underwear I got hooked on."

He plucks a color snapshot from a drawer and displays it. It shows Stafford Hartley in his overalls with a bra hooked around his waist. He grins. That's the underwear he's talking about. "My hips won't fit in the cups and the leg straps don't work right. The whole front end is wide open except for a flimsy belt and a no-hook buckle. That's the only way I'd ever write for them again is for them to run that picture and give me a front page apology. I can get meaner'n hell sometimes. Meaner'n hell. Proud of it."

He ponders that a minute before he says, "If I didn't give ol' Dick Nixon hell, who did?" And he is off again, rummaging through stacks of old newspapers, pulling out old columns. "Here's one. I was tryin' to double stink a stinkin' situation and they added one word and made it stink even worse than I stunk it." He produces another. "There's one that'll show you just how mean I am. I'll take any of 'em on. I'll take on the whole damn guv'ment single-handed. Hell, I'm one-eighth Indian."

He grins with satisfaction. "I'm purty damn mean, ain't I?"

Later, outside, absorbing the grand twilight vista from his porch, he isn't nearly so mean. "I'm of the mountains," he says softly. "I've traveled in 15 states and spent a month in Mexico and this is the truth, so help me, God: I've met good down-to-earth people wherever I've been, but I can get closer to God here in these mountains . . ."

For a while he is quiet.

"Seventy five years old. It's time to wear out." Then he grins. "I'm still not old. I admit I'm slightly aged around the middle, but I'm still not old. I've been a tough one, fella. And I can get meaner'n hell. Don't forget it. Meaner'n hell."

April, 1978
Bailey's Camp, North Carolina

Paula Sandburg
The Final Winter At Connemara

Morning. Clouds cling to hills stripped of autumn splendor by early winter, warm and wet. A great flock of grackles sweeps low through the hollow, wings beating the fog, as if whipping cream. Somewhere down off the Little River Road a hunter's shotgun KAAPLAMS and the rumble ripples away. Flat Rock, a summer village, is not yet astir.

Flat Rock is quietness, a subdued mountain village that long has attracted visitors from more hectic, less scenic places. One such visitor came to stay. His name was Carl Sandburg, peoples' poet, Lincoln biographer, teller of tales, singer of songs. He spent his last 22 years in Flat Rock.

Sandburg's home, a goat farm called Connemara, is just off the Little River Road, a big white house on the hill, difficult to see from the road even with the summer foliage gone. A narrow driveway twists up the hillside to the house through an archway of greenery: tall white pines 100 years old, rhododendron, laurel, spruces and hemlocks planted by Paula Sandburg, Carl's wife. The house defies a one-word architectural description. It was built more than 100 years ago by Christopher G. Memminger, secretary of the treasury for the Confederacy. There is a big front porch with white columns and on clear days, the porch offers a sweeping view of the blue-gray Smoky Mountains to the north. Sandburg loved the porch and spent many hours sitting there in a rough wooden chair talking with friends and visitors. In 1954 a national television audience sat with him as he picked his guitar and sang "Goober Peas" for Edward R. Murrow. It was the porch and its view that sold Connemara to the Sandburgs in 1945 when they came south from Michigan looking for a warmer climate and better pastures for their goats. Sandburg climbed the steps to the porch that first time, leaned against the rail and took in the view. "This is the place," he told his wife. "We will look no further."

Later, after the family moved in, Sandburg and his wife would sit on the porch absorbing a yellow-pink mountain sunset and Sandburg would turn to her and say, "Look at all the sky we bought," and they would both laugh.

167

Just Folks

In the cold morning mist, the empty porch gives no hint that it ever entertained such moments of warmth and happiness. At the side of the house, Paula Sandburg's old gray Chevrolet is parked. She doesn't drive anymore; her husband never did. A young woman's jeans, sneakers and underthings hang limp on a clothesline. The Sandburg dogs, Christina, a German shepherd, and Toni, offspring of Christina fathered by a black French poodle, bark and growl ferociously at visitors. They are, in fact, gentle. Beware the honking goose. He is not at all hospitable to strangers.

Paula Sandburg rises early. At 8 a.m. she is at the dining room table eating a grapefruit half and listening to the radio news from Asheville, 25 miles away. She frets about the Vietnam War, sits up for the final TV news at night and seldom misses the morning reports. She is a small woman, slightly stooped, with a kind of radiant face and wiry, unruly hair that she stretches into a bun at the back of her neck. At 84, she is a mountain flower, frail and lovely to the eye, yet seemingly as sturdy as the mountains themselves. She brims with laughter and youthfulness. "It's a funny thing," she says with a laugh, "the only time I know I'm old is when I look in the mirror."

Two of the Sandburgs' three daughters, Margaret and Janet, live in the 15-room house with their mother. The third, Helga, a poet and novelist, lives with her husband, a doctor, in Cleveland, Ohio. Helga's daughter, Paula, a vivacious woman of 24, with long blonde hair, has spent much of the fall and winter at Connemara working on a book of reminscences of her earlier years of the place. The clothes on the line are hers. So is the pet goose that jealously defends the hillside.

Paula Sandburg, her daughters and granddaughter are spending their final winter at Connemara. The National Park Service plans to preserve their home as an historic site. Mrs. Sandburg approves. It will be, she says, "a great park for the people." Soon the big house will be a museum with tourists trooping through listening to guides tell how and where her husband slept, worked and ate. One pasture will become a parking lot. And the wilderness trails that lace the Sandburgs' 243 acres spread over the mountains called Big and Little Glassy will see more people in a summer's month than they have for the past 100 years. "It will never be the same again," says granddaughter Paula, a bit wistfully.

For now, however, Connemara is still a home, a big comfortable home filled with the presence of Carl Sandburg, dead only six

months. He is still in every room. Books by him. Busts and paintings of him. Awards to him. And the photographs . . . Sandburg
laughing, singing, arguing, contemplating, picking flowers,
holding a baby goat, kissing a child. In the living room his
mellow guitar lies locked in its case atop the piano. In the study a
handful of yellow, fan-shaped ginkgo leaves are spread across a
desk.

"Mr. Sandburg always used to pick up some of them to keep for
the winter," his wife says of the leaves. "He really loved to pick
little things. Now not all men feel like picking a few flowers, but
he was always picking . . . you see different things around here,
you'd think it'd be maybe one of our kids that did it, but he
always brought things in."

At the center of the house is a room Mrs. Sandburg calls her
farm office. One wall is covered by the red and blue ribbons her
Chikaming goat herd won nearly 30 years ago. Another wall
bears a display of photographs of her husband, daughters and
grandchildren with her goats. Mrs. Sandburg delights in showing the pictures and telling about them. "There he is with all
these goats around him. And there he is with the first two goats
we ever bought. We bought four goats. First we bought two,
then we bought two more when he said, 'Why not get four,
enough to have our own butter?' "

The goats are gone now from Connemara. Mrs. Sandburg sold
them after her husband's death in July. But now she plans to try
to get some of the stock back, because the Park Service wants
Connemara to be as it was when Sandburg was alive. "I didn't
think they would want the goats," she says.

The goats were special to the whole family. The relationship
began when as a small child Helga, the eldest daughter, begged
her father for a cow. "Why do you want a big old cow?" Mrs.
Sandburg remembers her husband asking. "Why not a nice little
goat?" She laughs at the memory. At one point the herd
numbered several hundred. Only 60 remained at Sandburg's
death.

"He loved the kids," Paula Sandburg says. "That was the
reason, too, why we always brought the kids to the house. As
soon as they are born, if Mr. Sandburg is awake, I bring the kids
to him, because he wants to see what color they are. He was
always interested in seeing them. When they are real tiny . . ."
She laughs. ". . . We'd bring them in the dining room . . . by that
time they'd hop up in the air and kind of dance around then
come down again." Laughing, she holds out her arms and twirls

169

in imitation. "As cute as they could be. And they do more of that when they're real young, of that jumping up in the air, turning around and landing in a different direction. He loved to see that. So while he'd be eating dinner, you know, I'd bring the kids in and they would play around the dining room. So he was always close to them from the time they were born . . ."

Upstairs are Sandburg's bedroom and workroom, facing west. "You can't sell me an eastern exposure," Mrs. Sandburg recalls her husband saying. The reason was simple: he often worked through the night, didn't want the morning sun disturbing him. Mrs. Sandburg, not knowing when he had gone to bed, would put his breakfast — fruit and a Thermos of coffee — on a tray outside his door. The rooms are as he left them. Part of his collection of mountain walking sticks rests against a bedroom window sill. An eyeshade lies on a stack of records. Pictures Sandburg snipped from magazines, including one of himself, are tacked on one wall. There is a sink and beside it a bulky chest and on it an old-style Shick razor. As in the rest of the house, books are crammed floor to ceiling wherever there is room for shelves. Many bristle with bookmarks. A bedside table holds a conglomeration: books, magazines, sharpened pencils standing in a Regency beer can, a small gray figure of a hippopotamus, a box of Havana cigars, boxes of Chiclets, a blue muffler, a tin can filled with buckeyes from a tree up the mountain.

"Oh, he loved to bring the buckeyes," Mrs. Sandburg says. "We'd stop along there and there usually weren't many of them lying there, you know, we'd look just a little; he'd fill his pockets full of buckeyes."

The workroom adjoins the bedroom. "It's a dizzy corner," Sandburg once said of it, "kind of a crazy corner, because I don't pretend it's organized." It appears organized nevertheless. There are files and desks, a floor lamp, swivel chair, and a small table with an old, black portable typewriter. Notes in Sandburg's heavy-handed, almost unreadable scrawl are pinned on a board. An upended orange crate serves as a work bench. "He says it's just a handy size," Mrs. Sandburg says of the orange crate. "When we had our first home we had one of those. When we started having that home, we bought the few necessary things. We got a box that I fixed up for a dresser. We weren't going to spend a lot of money up there not even knowing how long we would stay there. We had some good Socialist friends who loaned us an extra they had they didn't need. We did have to buy us a stove, something like this . . ." She indicates the Dixie Flyer woodburner made of sheetmetal.

That Sandburg's tastes were simple and close to the working people is evident here. Reference materials are stuffed in cigar boxes and cardboard boxes bearing the labels of pork-and-beans, cranberry sauce, green peas. Anything that struck his fancy in newspapers and magazines, Sandburg clipped and saved, articles, photographs, drawings, jokes, quotes, Pogo comic strips (Pogo was his favorite comic character). Old machinery parts serve as paperweights. "He preferred something like that to something fancy. He was always interested in machinery. He knew nothing about machinery but he was always interested. He'd be in a factory, you know, he'd see something like that, you know, where they were lying around, he'd say, 'Do you need these things?' "

Sandburg had another favorite writing place when the weather was nice. It was behind the house, up the hill, where Little Glassy Mountain exposes some of its rocky gray innards to create a natural clearing in the trees. He had a big chair and a little table here, and just down the hill he kept a bench. He often would sit for hours, writing with heavy pencils on pocket notepads. "Nobody except the dogs came near him," Mrs. Sandburg says. The rock here is carpeted with moss, lichens and pine needles and the weathered chair sits now unused. The bench down the hill has collapsed, overtaken by vines. Paula Sandburg, looking through the mist at the bench, suddenly laughs at the memory of an incident that occurred years before.

"He disturbed a yellow jackets' nest when he was sitting around here. They almost ate him up. It was awful. We turned a hose on them . . . we happened to have a hose here . . . we turned that on and that chased the yellow jackets away."

Sandburg came to this rock to write much of his autobiography, *Always the Young Strangers*. Whenever he wanted to get away to think, his wife says, this is where he'd come. "Yes, he would do that. But usually, you know, he'd always have pads in his pockets. He'd get some ideas and then he'd have a notebook . . . He could work and write anywhere. Like for instance when we used to go from Elmhurst to Chicago, he tore books up. People said that was terrible for a man who loved books so much. He'd actually tear the book up so that he'd take a small section of the book with him and put it in his pocket and he'd read it. That's the way he got his reading done. I don't know why, he didn't want to carry a great big book into town, you know. He was a reporter. He had to have some little thing that

171

was inconspicuous. So many people said it was very peculiar that a man who loved books, you know, there'd be so many of his books that were torn up. The main thing is to get what's in the book into your head. There are some people that really a library is something to show off. And there are wealthy people who have beautiful libraries, all the best editions and everything, hardly ever look at any of them. Carl had just the opposite idea. With Carl a book was something to read, not something to look at. And if he had to tear it to pieces to read it, he would do it."

The light mist has become a steady, gentle rain, and Mrs. Sandburg, her voice already hoarse, hurries back inside. She sits at the dining room table watching a fat, fluffy bird gorge itself on sunflower seeds and peanut butter at a window feeding box, and she begins to talk about her husband's death at age 89.

"He always had a feeling . . . that, I think . . . that's why at the last, when he couldn't anymore, when he couldn't even, you know, take solid food, it was . . . he really, he had some bad weeks there, and that's the reason I was so resigned to his death, because to prolong that, to have more of that was . . . I didn't expect him to die though. I spoke to him at one o'clock in the morning. I came into the room, you know, and I bent over his bed there, and you see we had a nurse staying right with him, you know, and he looked at me and said, 'Paula.' You know, he was so happy to see me. I said, 'Now you'll want to sleep, won't you?' and then he fell back.

"And the nurse, you know, said that from then on he began breathing less, not such a vigorous breath, and so she was worried about him. Wasn't anything she could do about it though. Then another nurse came on in the morning, and the other nurse said, too, she noticed it too, that he wasn't breathing so deeply. So they called the doctor, and then the doctor came. 'Well, there's nothing we can do,' he said. And they were trying to give him artificial respiration. He said, 'There's no use in that,' because he felt, you know, his heart had stopped.

"Really, the tears that I shed were before that when he wasn't able really to enjoy life anymore, because this was . . . I was only thankful that it was an easy passing. You know, that he just breathed away. Everything had been very, you know . . . death is always difficult, but to have it come this way, so easily, just breathing away . . .

"He used to joke about his going to, you know, how long he was going to live and all that. But he wasn't frightened of death. Any man that had written all the poems he did about death — 'Finish,'

172

you know, let it come easy, you know, and he said not too much ceremony either, he said." She laughs. "He had written many poems about it. He knew he left enough behind him that he was really here when he was gone. I think of everything about him, but it doesn't make me feel sad. I think really, if he had died in a different way, if he had been suddenly cut down, that would have been different. But he suffered so much I'm just glad that he's dead, that's all I can say. I would hate to think that he had to keep on living . . . I know how he suffered there for those days, you know, so I just think that it's wonderful that he's relieved from it, that that's over and he didn't suffer any more than he suffered. And he's left himself. If anyone ever left himself still here on earth, it's he with his books. Especially to me with his poetry.

"He seems, I don't know, there's something about a man like my husband that put so much of himself into everything, that I really don't feel lonely. I just feel as though, and I don't have any superstitious feelings about it, I know that he's gone, but at the same time his spirit is with us, and he's going to live for America hundreds of years. There are many people who are going to feel he's still around, you know, a man who has put himself the way he has into books. He's really, he's really going to be around all the time. And there's so much of himself here."

For that reason, Paula Sandburg, who had thought of moving back north after her husband's death, will stay somewhere close to Flat Rock. "I decided this was the place for Carl to live out his years, and I think this may be the best place for me to live out my years, too."

The rain has stopped. Mrs. Sandburg walks down the winding driveway amongst trees and bushes she planted and others that have stood for more than 100 years. In other times, on warm summer nights with fireflies blinking down across the pastures, she had walked to the bottom of the hill with her husband and daughters, and at the bottom they all had clasped hands and climbed back to the big white house to sit on the porch in the quietness.

"This is what I fell in love with," she says, looking back up the hill toward the house. "This is really where my heart is . . . look at the stonework and the ivy growing on it. We put in these small hemlocks . . ."

For a few moments she stands quietly. "When I began to think of going away, I thought, who wants to go away from so lovely a place?"

Just Folks

That is why, when the Parks Service takes it over, she plans to stay close by. "I won't be spying on them, but I want to see how it's run. And then when we feel lonesome for this place, you know, we have so many ties to it, it won't be any trouble getting here."

January, 1968
Flat Rock, North Carolina

Paula Sandburg and her daughters moved from Connemara to nearby Asheville in 1968 and turned over their home to the National Park Service. Mrs. Sandburg died in February, 1977, after being bedridden four years. Connemara remains much as it was when she left it. The Park Service even returned some of her original goat herd to the farm. Connemara is open daily to visitors.

Stewart Simmons
Country Ham Man

Stewart Simmons slapped the pepper-coated ham onto the aging Sanitary scale, pierced it deftly with a long, sharp knife like a matador scoring the kill, then sniffed the knife blade and read the scale.

"There's a good'ern 'ere," he announced. "Nineteen and three quarter pound."

"I guess at 'em purty good," said his daddy, Charlie, who was only a few days away from being 81. It was Charlie who had just fetched the ham down the hill from the curing house. He leaned against the counter and grinned.

"Anybody 'ats got a sharp knife don't do nuthin', I always heered," said one of the locals, as he watched Stewart pierce the ham. He was propped against the drink box, killing time. Kidding Stewart Simmons is a local sport.

This is Simmons' Store. It is the center of commerce and community life for Triplett, a community of some 300 people which nestles in a valley along Elk Creek, just down the mountain from the Blue Ridge Parkway, about 10 miles east of Boone. Triplett is not on the beaten tourist path, but tourists by the hundreds make their way down the mountain and manage to find it, all of them drawn by the country hams Stewart Simmons cures each year and sells in his store.

The store is small and incredibly, magnificently cluttered. It is in the basement of Stewart's two-story, tin-roofed white house. Chickens scratch beneath the mimosas in the front yard. Bees manufacture honey in a row of white hives on the hill behind the house, honey that Stewart bottles and sells in his store. On weekends, the store is often as crowded as a shopping center supermarket.

Every weekend, Charlie Simmons stays busy leading a virtual parade of tourists and outlanders up the hill to the curing houses. There are three of them, each hanging full of hams saturated with salt, pepper, brown sugar, protected in white cloth sacks. Charlie takes pride in being able to pick the size ham a customer wants without being off more than a few ounces one way or the other.

175

Just Folks

Stewart stays busy inside the store, which doubles as Triplett's post office (Zip 28686).

"You reckon ol' El-Bee-Jay knows he's got a post office down here?" says an outlander, joining in the kidding, motioning to the corner of the store reserved for governmental transactions.

"Stewart, you got any good middlin' meat?" a local woman asks.

Stewart takes everything in stride without so much as a change of expression. He is a big man, age 53, with heavy-lidded eyes, a round bald spot, and an ample belly. When he does speak, he talks so fast many people can't understand him. He is often kidded about being a transplanted Yankee, sometimes by Yankee tourists, but he was born in Triplett and has remained here since, except for a brief spell during World War II.

If the people of Triplett ever had an election, Stewart Simmons probably would be elected to something. In addition to being storekeeper, ham curer and postmaster, he is also a lumber dealer, church and civic leader. His hams have helped pay for a community park and ball field and to put brick on the little Baptist church down the road.

Stewart opened his store when he was still in school. It once occupied one of the small outbuildings, now plastered with snuff and soft drink signs, beside the house. He moved it into the basement in 1942, when he became postmaster.

"Started curing hams in '39," he said. "Took 'em down country to sell 'em. They come and get 'em anymore."

He raised his own hogs and killed them to cure his first hams. He cured 26 hams and took 25 of them down to Mooresville to see if he could sell them. They went fast at 25¢ a pound. The next year, he raised even more hogs, cured more hams, and the following year even more. After that, he didn't have to take the hams down country anymore. People were beginning to come after them, and Stewart had to start buying fresh hams to cure from local farmers just to meet the demand.

He never advertised. Word about his hams just passed somehow. Tourists discovered them. People from New York, Cleveland, Chicago came once, then returned every year on their vacations. They took back not only hams but the fresh honey that Stewart bottled and the bell pepper jelly and fruit preserves his mother made. He has regular customers from a dozen different states.

"Guy from Spain came in here and got one, one time," he said. "Got two, in fact."

Stewart's ham business grew until he was selling thousands every year and the local farmers could no longer keep him supplied with enough hams to cure. So when curing time comes, around Thanksgiving, refrigerated trucks roll down the mountain bringing loads of fresh hams from packing houses in the midwest. Even the mountain country hams are tourists nowadays.

September, 1968
Triplett, North Carolina

Aunt Doshie
Late Cucumbers

The dirty, blue Volkswagen crawled up the red mountain road and stopped at a mailbox. Stewart Simmons, belly bulging, trousers bagging, unfolded from the front seat, loped the few feet to the mailbox and wrestled it open. He took out a big brown envelope and a newspaper and looked them over as he returned to the car.

Just a trace of a road led off the mountainside, double tracks of red dirt and rocks grown over with weeds, disappearing into a treeline. Simmons nosed the little car into the fender-high weeds, and, lurching and groaning, it started the climb. Halfway up the hillside, a startled pheasant darted from the weeds and raced wildly into the rhododendron thicket alongside a narrow, clear stream.

"You see that?" Simmons asked.

The old house loomed from the weeds near the top of the hill. Unpainted, grayed by weather, tin-roofed, it would have been a typical mountain farm home half a century earlier. It has stood much longer than that. The last addition to it was made in 1908. Now, lost in the weeds, it looked deserted and lonely.

Simmons whipped the car out into a field, pushing down the high weeds, then backed and aimed it back down the mountain before stopping and opening his door. "Old lady lives here all by herself," he said.

On the back porch, a fly swam in a bucket of fresh spring water. "Doshie!" called Simmons, stepping onto the porch. "Hey, Doshie!"

The voice from inside was muffled. Simmons pushed open the heavy door. It was dark inside, and the room had a chill. Except for the telephone on a low table by the stone fireplace, the room was from another era, piled high with the clutter of a long lifetime. A wood range, covered with utensils, stood in one corner. A small table loaded with dishes and food was pushed against a wall. The late summer harvest was in: dishpans filled with dried, shelled beans sat about. A box of newly dug potatoes and basketful of unshucked yellow corn sat in the floor. An old, long rifle rested by the door.

178

Aunt Doshie, as she is called by those who know her, sat by the cold ashes in the fireplace, a picture from the past. She wore a bonnet, an apron over skirts that reached the floor. She was pretty once, and her eyes are still bright. But her back is grotesquely bent now and her face is as weathered as the old house. A few strands of white hair hung from beneath the bonnet. She took the mail and said she had been feeling poorly.

"How old are you now, Doshie?" Simmons asked.

"Eighty three and a third."

"How long since Uncle Jim died?"

"Eighteen years last April," she said.

"Y'all set down, Stewart."

"We got to be getting on back down the hill," he said. "We just stopped by for a minute."

Aunt Doshie got to her feet to clear a sitting place. She moved a pan of peas from a woodblock and cleaned a straight-back chair. We made motions to leave. "Nice to have met you," I said.

"Don't y'all leave, Stewart," she said. "Please set down and talk awhile."

"We got to get on," he said, pausing to finger the potatoes in the cardboard box. "You dig these?"

"Yes. I got some more out there but I ain't been able to dig 'em. I guess the field mice will eat 'em."

We went outside. "Stewart," Aunt Doshie called. "I wish y'all would stay. Do y'all eat cucumbers?"

"Where'd you get cucumbers this time of year?" he asked, going back inside.

He emerged shortly carrying two big cucumbers that had already begun to turn yellow. "Y'all need salt?" Aunt Doshie called after him.

"No, we're not goina eat 'em now."

As the car bounced back down the mountainside, Simmons talked about Aunt Doshie's children, the three still living. One, he said, has a big government job in Washington. None comes back to visit often.

"Does anybody come up here to see her?" I asked.

"No."

"Who looks after her?"

"I come up and check on her ever' now and then. I got to get her some wood before bad weather sets in."

"She must get awfully lonely," I said.

"She's happy," he said.

September, 1968
Triplett, North Carolina

179

Donald McCourry
The Author from Dog Flat Hollow

He remembers well the day they came. He was working at a furniture factory in Lenoir then. He came home for lunch and the package was there. "I took 'em out and they looked awful good," he recalls.

That was two years ago, and for Donald L. McCourry it was a proud and triumphant moment. In his hands he now holds a book, *Us Poor Folks And the Things Of Dog Flat Hollow*, by Donald L. McCourry. Quite an achievement for a young mountain man who attended school only a day and a half in his youth, who didn't learn to read and write until he was 17.

But now he looks back at that moment, at his achievement and says, "At times I do regret it. I don't know if that's the right thought, but at times I do regret it."

Donald McCourry is 32 now. He was born in Erwin, Tennessee, a small town close to the North Carolina line. For the first two and a half years of his life, he was passed from hand to hand until he was taken in by his mother's childless cousin and her husband, Sena and Aspie McCourry, mountain people. The McCourrys lived in a log cabin in a hollow called Dog Flat in the Pigeon Roost section of Mitchell County near the village of Relief, about 12 miles from the town of Bakersville, the county seat. They lived in self-sufficiency without electricity, plumbing or automobile. Their meager income came from gathering wild herbs and raising burley tobacco.

When Donald was old enough to go to school, the McCourrys moved into a new log house Aspie McCourry had built closer to the road. But on the second day of school, Donald had to be taken out.

"Nerves," he says. "When I'd get away from my parents, I'd just go all to pieces. I'd start crying."

He never returned to school. He was extraordinarily shy and sickly, susceptible to asthma attacks and nosebleeds. He learned his ABCs at home with the help of a couple of books a teacher had given his mother. Those were the only books in the house, except for the Bible, and Donald didn't learn to read and write until he was 17, when a neighbor, Harvey J. Miller, gave him a dictionary.

Harvey Miller wrote a column of local news for the newspaper in Erwin, Tennessee, and he asked Donald to help supply items from the Pigeon Roost area. Soon Donald was writing his own column, the "Byrd Creek News Tidings." He had a fascination with big and exotic words, and he liberally salted his column with them, usually misused, but the editor ran the column as he wrote it. In one column he reported: "Conway Hughes here on Byrd Creek reported to the writer that he had seen one day last week an Aardvark on the mountain over from his door. Mr. Hughes said the Aardvark came down the hill about 4:30 p.m. It was the first one he had seen this winter . . ." In the dictionary, Donald had come across the word aardvark and been taken with it. He saw that it came from Dutch, meaning earth pig. " 'Earth' is ground, and 'pig' is hog," he explains, "Aardvark sounded better to me than groundhog."

He built himself a tiny log cabin he called his news office and there he struggled with words, learned to operate a camera, even set up a crude printing operation. Eventually, he also wrote local news columns for newspapers in Spruce Pine and Burnsville. In 1965, when Donald was 19, a vacationing magazine editor from Philadelphia, Barbara Bennett Talley, read one of his columns and began corresponding with him. She urged him to write a book about his life, offered to help get it published if he did.

Donald was reluctant, uncertain of his writing. He gave up writing for newspapers when he was 20 and had to leave Dog Flat Hollow seeking work. He had little time for writing books. He worked at several different jobs in different places before settling into a furniture factory job in Lenoir after his marriage in 1971. He had done no writing in those years, but he had continued his correspondence with Barbara Talley. Four years ago, he took her advice and began writing the story of his youth in the mountains. He wrote it mostly at night after working all day in the furniture factory. "I pushed myself for two years," he says.

The book was published in November, 1975. It was a candid book, "written in my own phraseology," filled with innocence and details of the hard and simple mountain life, well-dosed with fancy words. For a few weeks, it seemed it might do well. But within a few months of his book's publication, the author was not doing so well. The book's sales rapidly dwindled and produced only a small amount of royalties. His real mother took exception to parts of the book in a lengthy letter. He had the feeling other people mentioned in it didn't like what he had written. Although most reviews were favorable, some were critical, and that was difficult for him to handle (he had quit jobs because of criticism). He began feeling the effects of having pushed himself so hard to finish the book. "I started breaking down," he says. "I got to feeling so bad at the time that I couldn't hardly go."

Four months after his book came out, he lost his job. That was almost two years ago. He hasn't worked since. He moved his family to a rented house about a mile down the mountain from Interstate 40 on the edge of the small town of Nebo, about halfway between Morganton and Marion. His family gets welfare help, food stamps. It isn't easy for Donald McCourry to accept.

He sits now by the wood fire, looking at his book and speaking of regrets. "Overall, I guess it's a good thing. But if I had it to do over again, I'd do a lot of rewriting. I feel like a snake in the spring of the year after it's crawled out of its wintershed. In a way, it's like me, and in a way it's not. At the time I wrote it, I felt different than I do now."

He has done no more writing. "I want to write if I can get someone to accept it. I got pretty low hopes . . . I kinda have a handicap in writing. Getting all the words in the right place and using the right word is my handicap."

He talks now of maybe going back to Dog Flat Hollow, building a log house, trying to make a go of it as his parents did. If he does, one thing will be different for his children. In one room of the small house, the walls are covered, floor to ceiling, with shelves, and the shelves are filled with books — reference books, classics, popular novels, hundreds and hundreds of volumes.

Donald McCourry's wife, Sarah, stands in the room watching their two children, Deborah, five, and Omar, three, romping at play. "If they don't learn," she says, "it won't be because they didn't have a chance."

"If I'd had all these when I was growing up," says her husband, "I might've come to something."

January, 1978
Nebo, North Carolina

Joe McKennon
Circus Boss

The wagon wheels on the fence at the foot of the driveway are not the typical decorative wagon wheels seen at many mountain homes. These are gaily painted. Circus wagon wheels.

"There are few people left that know anything about the old-time circus," Joe McKennon said. "I'm one of the very few, you see."

Joe McKennon is a powerful looking man with white hair and chiseled features and a gruff, rumbling voice that was made for giving commands. He was sitting in the rambling house he built on a mountainside with his own hands. The room had a wallful of windows from which he could look out over a large portion of his sprawling farm to the blue mountains on the horizon. Joe McKennon was reminiscing.

"I ran away with my first circus when I was 12 years old, because they didn't have seats on the hoe handles in the cotton patch," he said with a grin. His father, a Tennessee farmer, came after him. "They put me back in the cotton patch, but they didn't do any good with me. I would sell this farm tomorrow if cotton would sprout on it."

Two years later, he ran off with a carnival because he'd fallen in love with a ball game queen named Mable. His parents came after him again. They might just as well have let him go, for Joe McKennon was intent on spending his life with the circus.

"When I was three years old, I told my folks that was what I was going to do," he said. "I was born with it. If you're not born with it, you better stay away from it."

Boll weevils wiped out the McKennon farm, and his father moved the family to Texas where he became a railroad man. Joe quit school and began an apprenticeship as a coach builder for the Sante Fe. At the age of 19, his apprenticeship behind him, he left a comfortable salary with the railroad and took a 50 per cent cut in pay to repair coaches for the American Circus Corporation, which operated five big train circuses out of Indiana. He was at last where he wanted to be.

The appeal of the circus to Joe McKennon never lay in the glamour and glory of the spotlight. With him, it was logistics.

183

Striking those big tents and moving all that equipment along with animals and people everyday, then setting up again in another town — that was what he enjoyed. His plan was to learn every angle of the circus business, and he set out to do just that, moving from the blacksmith shop to selling candy and tickets, to working the front entrance to serving as head usher — all the jobs, until he got to be boss. He was born to boss. Anybody need only look at him to see that.

"We had a caste system stronger than any military caste system," he said. "We were the last survivors of the sailing ship days. No big canvasses were ever handled without a certain amount of profanity and brutality." Joe McKennon never hesitated to use either. "That thing has been knocked back to here many times," he said, doubling his massive fist back to his wrist. "It was rough. It was rough and tough." Bosses were hated and feared and sometimes killed by their own men. "If you had a white guy in your crew who could lay you out, then you were out and *he* was the boss," he recalled. Joe McKennon remained the boss.

Oftentimes, there were others to battle as well. Local roughnecks, "town sucks" the circus people called them, would come out and try to cut the ropes and drop the tent, and then there would be battles with iron stakes and whatever other weapons were available. There were coal mining towns in Kentucky that could always be counted on for a fight. "We'd battle off the lot every time we played those towns."

In the '30s, when the circus business began to fade, Joe McKennon went over to bossing carnivals for a while. Then the war came along and stopped that. He tried to get into the Air Corps and was rejected, so he went off to be carpentry foreman at a powder plant until the Army finally took him. He worked in Army Ordinance and later designed and built the shipping crates for the "Fat Boy," one of the atomic bombs dropped on Japan. After the war, Joe McKennon returned to Tennessee with a new bride and began to put together a tent show. The idea was to take Broadway to Main Street, staging three different plays under the big tent.

"Yeah," he said, "we were taking Broadway to Main Street and they didn't give a damn whether Broadway came to Main Street or not. We showed to an average of 69 people every night.

When he switched to comedy and a country band, the show became a success and he kept it on the road for four years before tiring of it. He came to the mountains of North Carolina then and bought a dairy farm. He quickly doubled the farm's production, innovating several new farming techniques in the process. He doesn't farm anymore, however. His energies are again devoted to the circus. He spends winters now in Sarasota, Florida, where he donates his services to the Ringling Museum of the Circus, restoring old wagons and creating displays.

One room of Joe McKennon's house is itself a circus museum, crammed with memorabilia, and it is here that he is writing his circus book, a novel about the early days that he plans to call *The Horse Dung Trail*. "Well, that's what it was," he said. "We all followed it for a number of years."

Those were the days he liked most. "When we got rid of the horses, I really wasn't interested in it anymore. But you know we have as many tented circuses today as we've had in the last 40 years."

Would he like to be back with them again? "Actually no. All I have to do is go visit once in a while, watch them struggle to get it up, see the shortage of help . . . actually there's not too much showmanship . . . and I just lose my desire to be around it."

July, 1974
Fletcher, North Carolina

Milada Thurmond
Innkeeper

The last of the supper crowd was just beginning to depart before Milada Thurmond found time to take a breather from the kitchen and cool herself in a rocking chair on the front porch. It really was a sort of curtain call for her, because all the diners had something good to say about the meal as they left.

She thanked them all, insisting that it wasn't anything special. Just one of her regular weeknight spreads. There had been homemade vegetable beef soup for a starter, followed by gelatin fruit salad, peach halves and cottage cheese, pickled peaches, cucumbers, watermelon rinds, pickled corn and macaroni salad. There had been platters of barbecue chicken, heaps of roast beef with brown gravy, big bowls of creamed corn, green beans, beets, lima beans and Milada's famous crunchy buttered apples. There had been biscuits hot from the oven and freshly baked butternut squash pie. All were served family-style at the price of $5 per person. Just a regular weeknight spread. Nothing like her Sunday buffets when she bakes big turkeys, cooks three or four more meats and many more vegetables, plus several salads. That's only four bucks.

"I didn't ever think about cooking," she said. "Everybody thinks my biscuits are better than theirs, but they aren't any better. You just get 'em when they come out of the stove. I make 'em as they eat 'em. I never been trained to cook. I just cook like my mama cooked."

Milada has been cooking for a long time. She is the owner and operator of the Phelps House, a big white house on a hill that has been taking in lodgers for nearly 100 years. She has owned it only for the past 10, however. For many years, she and her husband had a truck stop in Georgia. She reared a family while cooking three meals a day for the truckers, washing their trucks and pumping diesel fuel. "I've washed many a truck for five dollars," she said. "Now you have to pay five dollars to get your car rinsed off."

She worked long and hard and never had a chance to go anywhere or see anything. When her daughter went off to

187

Just Folks

Hawaii to study in the early '60s, Milada decided she was just going to Hawaii and visit her. She got stranded there by an airlines strike and couldn't have been happier. She was captivated by Hawaii. "The water over there is so blue and beautiful," she said, more than a little wistfully, "and the sand won't even stick to your feet. You know, those girls over there, they go to dancing and singing and they got one muumuu and they tell you that the best things in life are free and you go to believing it."

Most things weren't free, however, not by a long shot. She sat down one day for lunch in one of the Honolulu hotels and ate a green salad with a little bacon crumbled in it that cost her $6.50. At that time, back in Georgia, she was selling meals of meat, four vegetables, sliced tomatoes, coffee or tea and pie for 88¢. "I'm going home and sell my business and come back over here and open me an eating place," she told her daughter.

She was just kidding, but a few years later, after her husband died and she discovered she couldn't run the truck stop alone, she decided that was precisely what she was going to do.

At that time, her sister, Evona, had owned the Phelps House for many years and given it her maiden name. Her six sisters came every summer to stay with her for a while. When Milada came to tell her she was going off to Hawaii to live, Evona tried to talk her into buying the Phelps house instead.

"In five minutes I had changed my mind," Milada said. "I didn't go to Honolulu. I still think it would be fun to live there, though."

Anyway, she liked the North Carolina mountains almost as much as she liked the blue waters and unsticky sands of Hawaii. "I think this is the best climate in the United States. And it's so pretty here. Have you ever been up here in the winter? When it goes to snowing in these mountains and all those leaves are off the trees, it looks like a beautiful white satin wedding gown has been thrown over these mountains."

She soon was cooking three meals a day and word spread quickly about her cooking. Sometimes, when she opened the doors, there would be people lined up down the street waiting to enter.

One of the things she liked to do was decorate her dining room in accordance with the season and for special events and holidays. One day in the summer of 1973, she was standing on a table putting up an apple tree when she fell, and a sharp table corner penetrated her back. "I had 35 people in the house and I told my daughter just to send them all home and close the door," she recalled. Her daughter chose to try to keep the place open and called a sister-in-law from Georgia to help.

"She was up here and stayed 10 days and she had to go back and stay in bed two months from doing what I was doing," Milada said with a laugh.

For those 10 days Milada was in the hospital, and later she had to return for 10 more. The first day she was out, she was back in her kitchen. "I just told myself, I know good and well I'm made of better stuff than this. That night I came in, I cooked 1,100 biscuits holding onto the table."

That very night a man came in and asked if she might be interested in selling the place. His timing couldn't have been better. In the fall of 1973, she closed the Phelps House, bought a little house out on the Dillard Highway and retired. She was 63 at the time.

"I had worked all my life and I decided I'd travel. I went everywhere in the world I ever wanted to go. But, you know, when you buy your coffee in Miami and your cream and sugar in Canada, you money soon runs out. I had spent more money in one month than I had intended to spend in a year."

While she traveled, the new owner transformed the Phelps House into a "gourmet restaurant" with a fancy name. By the fall of 1975, the restaurant had failed, the new owner had defaulted and departed, and Milada Thurmond found herself in possession of the old place again.

It was a wreck. All the furniture had been sold. Even her big kitchen stove was gone. She kept finding garlic bulbs hanging all around the place. She already had made her decision: she was going to reopen the place as it had been before. "I told my daughter, 'We're going to have the biggest Thanksgiving dinner that's ever been held in Highlands'." And she did, too.

She has just recently begun getting the place back to the way it once was, and word is beginning to spread that she has returned and reopened. She still cooks three meals a day for guests who lodge with her (the price for a room and three meals is still less than the cost of a room at a lot of other places), but the dining room is now open to others only for the evening meal. Her back won't allow her to cook the way she used to for big crowds at all three meals. "I don't guess my back will ever be the same. I could lift a bedstead before I fell."

Still, she gets up at 6:30 every morning to start cooking and she stays in the kitchen well into the night; but it doesn't bother her, she says, and she has no plans to quit again. "I'm not going to sell it anymore. I'm just going to stay here 'till I drop. I wasn't happy retired. It's not what you think it is."

On their way out, some of the diners wanted to know what she was planning to cook for the following evening. "I don't know what I'm going to have tomorrow night," she told them. "I never plan anything. Up here on top of the mountain, you cook whatever you get your hands on."

She couldn't sit long enjoying the coolness. She got up to go back inside, back to the kitchen. "I've got five bushels of peaches out there to peel yet tonight," she said. "They sure have eat up a lot of peach cobbler around here lately."

July, 1976
Highlands, North Carolina

Bascom Lamar Lunsford
Minstrel Of the Appalachians

Age has done its cruel and relentless work on Bascom Lamar
Lunsford. He's 90 now and he can't pick the banjo nor dance
anymore, and he doesn't like it at all.

He suffered a stroke back in 1965 that caused him to miss the
Mountain Folk and Dance Festival for the first time since he
founded it in 1928. The doctor told him he might be able to attend
that year, but he definitely wouldn't be able to dance. "If I can't
dance," snorted Lunsford, "there's no use in going."

Now he spends his days propped up on a sofa in a small apartment in West Asheville. He had to move from his home on South
Turkey Creek (a house that was always open to fiddlers, banjo
pickers, ballad singers, cloggers and visiting dignitaries) to be
nearer his doctors and other conveniences. He is a little man, frail
and pale, with flaring eyebrows. He still dresses in dark suits and
big black bowties, as he always did. But his hands shake now
when he tries to hold a banjo; he's grown hard of hearing, and his
memory fails him now and then. "I'm just sorry I've got to be as
old as I am. It's just terrible to be 90 years old," he said. "I've been
fighting this stroke from a few years back, but I believe I could
get out here and take a turn. I believe I could . . ."

In his long life, Bascom Lamar Lunsford has been teacher,
lawyer, salesman, court solicitor, congressional campaign chairman — but an early love, the culture of the mountain people,
became his life's true work. "My business was to draw attention
to the fine cultural value of our traditional music and our dancing
and the fine honor of our people . . ." he said. "I was trying to
perpetuate the real true cultural work of the mountain people.
Our section, you know, has been slandered . . ."

As a boy growing up near Asheville, Lunsford learned to play
the banjo, and he and his brother even made their own instruments. Later, he became a salesman for a nursery, peddling
apple trees throughout the mountains. Sometimes he'd trade
them for songs. The job gave him the chance to visit a lot of
mountain cabins ("I've been in more mountain homes than
anybody you can think of . . ."), and he always got around to asking his hosts if they knew any songs. The thing he looked for was

"a plain tale, simply told" put to song. He collected songs wherever he went. He catalogued thousands and set many to memory. He later recorded some for the Library of Congress, Columbia University and two commercial recording companies.

Lunsford's interest in the mountain culture took him all over the country, playing his banjo, reciting songs, speaking, presenting mountain performers he had discovered. He took some of those performers to Europe for an international folk festival, and the group was invited to the White House to perform for King George VI of England and his queen. "When we got back," he recalled with a chuckle, "everybody asked me, 'What did the queen say?' I said, 'She just sat there and patted her foot'."

In the hopes of preserving the mountain culture and encouraging others to learn about and appreciate it, Lunsford founded the Mountain Folk and Dance Festival in Asheville. He later organized similar festivals in Renfro Valley, Kentucky, at the University of North Carolina, and the North Carolina State Fair. He played a leading role in organizing the first National Folk Festival in St. Louis and remained active in the annual festival throughout its existence. The Asheville festival is the oldest of its type in the country and the one that is closest to Lunsford's heart. It is held the first week in August in Asheville's City Auditorium, and it has always been a rather informal affair. "In 46 years, I've never had a written program, never had a piece of paper in my hand," Lunsford said. "I knew the fellers, knew what they played, knew how well they did it, you see." He was always a purist about his music. Nothing modern allowed, nobody wearing cowboy hats and playing "country and western," no imitation folk singers from New York wearing beards and beads. "Go natural. I've stuck to that straight through. I won't caricature the mountain folks."

Eventually, organizing and promoting the festival became a full-time job for Lunsford. "In the beginning, I'd practice law and do these things as I could, as I went along. But I couldn't afford to have my clients telling the judge, 'He's off somewhere picking the banjo.' " So he gave up law.

The festival is now under the direction of his son, Lamar, but Lunsford still attends, as he has every year except the year he had his stroke, even though he can't dance. "I go over there and sit backstage and talk to my friends and all. I go out on stage just a little, just long enough to give it the color — and to keep from falling off stage." He smiled and confessed he always liked to be on stage. "When I was four years old, I'd recite little jingles and so on, and they'd carry me out to the school on Fridays to recite and I got the feel of how it was to please an audience. I got that feel. Well, I have it yet."

He always could stir an audience. He knew what they wanted. And he had a flair for promotion. He would latch onto little things, such as calling himself the Minstrel of the Appalachians, or the Squire of South Turkey Creek, and really promote them. He was never bashful about promoting himself — he figured he had to do it to accomplish his goals — and he was quite successful at it. He and his festival got attention all around the world, and he never spent a dime on advertising.

One time, Bascom Lamar Lunsford tried his own hand at songwriting, and he was successful at that, too. He wrote "Old Mountain Dew" about 1920, and it became a classic. "Yes sir. It's still alive. It's a good'un yet." The song is a ballad with a moral; he wouldn't have written it otherwise. He wrote it, he said, because he felt sorry for the mountain boys who got taken in by slickers. These guys would set them up in the moonshine business and then disappear when the mountain boys got caught.

"I never made any blockade likker in my life," he said, "but I've seen them do it. I've been there. A fellow running a still might have a song, you know."

He sat now, propped on the pillows on his sofa and recited "Old Mountain Dew," every verse of it. "Now that's the way I made it and sung it way back yonder," he said when he finished. "I set down 350 songs from personal memory. I can remember most of them now like I did 'Old Mountain Dew.' I have a mighty good memory, but it fails me sometimes now."

He looked back on his life, considered it, and pronounced himself satisfied. "I wanted to do something worthwhile and I think I've done that." His greatest accomplishment, he said, was convincing people that there was value in the culture of the mountain people. "People had a notion that it was somehow inferior. Now they've turned around and found there might be something in it. The interest in it has been very, very good . . . And I've established a lot of friends. I don't know of any enemies I've made. And I've had more fun than anybody you ever saw."

March, 1972
Asheville, North Carolina

Bascom Lamar Lunsford died in September, 1973. His Mountain Folk and Dance Festival is still held each summer in Asheville.

193

Ted and Hester Sutton
Professional Hillbillies

The days are gone when Ted and Hester Sutton used to back up traffic, sometimes for a mile and a half and more, on U.S. Highway 19. There they would be on the porch: Ted with his long gray beard and hillbilly hat, his bear claw around his neck, his loaded .38 on his hip, and his banjo on his knee; and Hester, all done up in her bonnet and long dress; the two of them rocking away.

It was a rare tourist indeed who did not stop to see them. They were the personification of Maggie Valley. Hester was called Maggie; Ted was Maggie's Old Man. Ted would pick his banjo, and sometimes the two of them would dance mountain dances. Always they posed for pictures. Over all the long summers that they worked the tourists, Ted and Hester figure they must have had a million snapshots taken of them. And Ted was always quick to remind the picture takers that he and Hester weren't amateur hillbillies. "Got a little donation, you'll give me?" he'd say. "Takes money to ride the train, you know . . ."

Up in Evans Cove, the family still gathers to talk and laugh about how Granny and Gran'paw, as they call Ted and Hester, used to hustle the tourists. And Ted, 77 now and frail after two years of sickness, still marvels over how he used to haul rocks down from the creek and sell them to gullible tourists, pricing them, naturally, according to size.

It seemed to Ted those tourists would buy anything. They tried to buy his hat, his bear claw, his banjo, and just about everything else. He figured he could have sold himself to some of them, if he'd been of a mind to, and just got in the car with them and gone on off to Florida or Ohio or someplace. It seemed, too, that they'd believe anything. He and Hester still can't get over all the questions they'd ask.

"Ever' kind of question in the world," says Hester. "They's even people come up and ask how long the mountains been there."

"I told 'em them big mountains had been there for three weeks," says Ted, "and I'as goin' over to Tennessee and git me some little'uns and bring 'em back."

"They was somebody asked him where the road went to," says granddaughter Becky Sue Green, "and he said, 'I don't know; it's there when I go to bed at night and it's still there when I git up in the mornin'.'"

"Would any of the purty women come along and ask you to date 'em, Daddy?" asks his daughter, Ina Rich, with whom he now lives.

"No, but I danced with a many of 'em."

"You wuz wantin' that dollar, wudn't you, Gran'paw," says Hester, laughing.

Ted and Hester, who is now 70, have spent most of their lives in Maggie Valley. Both were born in the area, and Ted was raised, along with the beans, potatoes, corn and cabbages his father grew, on the top of Buck Mountain; his family homeplace is now occupied by an amusement park called Ghost Town. As a young man, Ted farmed, logged, drove cattle. He picked the banjo for fun. He can't remember now when he learned to play it. "I just been pickin' a little all my life," he says.

"He just picked that banjer up," says his daughter, Ina. "It was in 'im, you know."

After Ted and Hester were married 56 years ago and started raising their eight children (all of whom are still living), Ted took whatever work he could find. He worked on the construction of Fontana Dam, operated a jackhammer digging a seven-mile tunnel through a mountain at Waterville to divert the Pigeon River. When he couldn't find work, he prowled the mountains digging ginseng ('sang, he calls it). Twice, he had to leave the mountains to find work, once in a shipyard in Newport News and another time in Florida, picking oranges. Both times he couldn't wait to get back home. "I'm just a hillbilly back in the mountains," he says.

It wasn't until about 20 years ago, though, that Ted became a professional hillbilly. The tourists had been pouring through Maggie Valley for about 10 years then. Cherokee on the other side of Soco Gap had its Apache-feathered chiefs to attract attention, but Maggie Valley had no such gimmick. So Ted went to work as a banjo-picking hillbilly at the Maggie Country Store, and it worked. His services were soon in demand by other businesses. "I played at about every craft shop up that valley," he says.

As the crowds grew larger, Ted saw he ought to have a place of his own. So he bought a piece of land on the highway and built a hillbilly house out by the road. There on the porch, summer after summer, he and Hester worked the tourists. They had a little crafts shop in the house, a corndog stand on the side, and they converted an old barn out back into a theater where they staged country music shows at night. "Oh, we made a lot of money there," says Ted. "Oh boy."

"We made a lot," adds Hester, "but we spent it."

The money didn't come easy. Seven days a week, daylight to dusk, Ted and Hester worked on the porch, picking and dancing and posing, then moved back to the barn for the nighttime shows. And sometimes, especially at night, things got rough. Ted didn't wear his .38 just for show. He once shot a beer can out of the hand of a man who was about to attack him, he says.

"Yeah, you can have trouble anywhere in the world there's music. Where there's music, there's likker, you know."

"Nobody didn't mess with Gran'paw," says Becky Sue.

"They didn't mess with me neither," says Hester. "I kept me a billy hangin' on the porch. If they messed with me I'd take that billy and knock the fire out of 'em."

Hester and Ted worked their last full summer together in 1974. The following year, Ted fell ill with breathing difficulties, the result, he says, of dust he breathed when he was building that tunnel through the mountain years earlier. Infections set in and, nearly dying, he was hospitalized. After coming out of the hospital an invalid, his hands stiffened so he no longer could play the banjo.

"Oh, he went crazy," says Ina. "We had to hide the guns and everything."

Ted's and Hester's Hillbilly Fun House is still in business each summer, operated by a daughter, Myrtle Nolan. Shows are held in the barn out back, but there is no corndog stand anymore, and no crafts shop selling creek rocks to tourists. Instead, there is a small campground that attracts hillbilly music lovers who gather on the porch to play or sing or listen. There are no longer traffic jams waiting to get into the place, but frequently people will stop to inquire of Myrtle Nolan whatever happened to Maggie and Maggie's Old Man.

Ted never goes to the place anymore. Once, thinking it might help him, his family took him there to sit on the porch for a while, but he wanted to leave after just a few minutes. I ask him if he misses it, and he looks down and says, "Yeah, I guess I do."

Not Hester. "I'm glad," she says. "I wouldn't have it back at all. When we used to run that, I'd lay down at night and I could hear the banjers and g'itars and fiddles in my sleep. It gits on me. I go down there now and hear a little bit of that and my stomach just goes to quiverin' and shakin' plumb to my back. I have to take my nerve medicine."

Up in Evans Cove now, Ted spends much of his time listening to a 24-hour-a-day country music radio station. Sometimes he sits in the front door of his daughter's small house looking at Buck Mountain rising magnificently before him and listening to the gunshots from the cowboy fights being staged on the mountain-top where he spent his boyhood. For a long time his family was worried about him, but on his birthday in May, he got up and did a little dance, and that was the first sign to his family that he might be on his way to recovery.

As I start to leave, after visiting with the family for several hours, I ask Ted and Hester if I might take a picture of them. They agree, but first Ted insists on getting his bear claw and hanging it around his neck over his pajama top. Hester leads him out into the front yard and Becky Sue calls, "Look purty, Gran'paw." She stands back smiling. "He'd rather have his picture made than anything."

I snap several pictures. Ted looks at me and grins. "Got a little donation you'll give me?" he says. "Takes money to ride the train . . ."

His watching family laughs and beams, for this is another good sign.

July, 1977
Maggie Valley, North Carolina

Amoneeta Sequoyah
Medicine Man

Usually it isn't the Indians who come but others, white folks. Some have driven great distances and some are desperate. They have heard of him somehow, usually by word of mouth, and they come to seek his help. To them he is known as Chief Running Wolf, but the locals from whom they are apt to ask directions call him Doc Sequoyah.

Following the directions they get from the locals, the visitors take the river road into Big Cove, where the Cherokee Reservation backs into the Great Smoky Mountains National Park. And if they take the proper turn onto the rocky, unpaved road that strikes out up the mountainside, they soon come to the sign: "Medicine Man's Hut."

It isn't a hut at all, just another of the modern house trailers that have in the past few years begun replacing the tar paper shanties on the reservation. A porch and a small, crudely constructed wooden room have been added to the front of the trailer. The room was added for the herbs.

Dogs and children wander freely through the trailer's open door and inside, seated beneath a strand of flypaper bearing so many corpses that other suicide-bent flies seem to be having trouble finding a landing spot, is a tall, lean man whose dark, deeply set eyes are at once blank and all-knowing. His name is Amoneeta Sequoyah. He wears cowboy-style clothes, and he looks at least 15 years younger than his 74 years.

"See," he is saying, "I'm the only Indian living that was born a medicine man. I was *born* a medicine man."

It was not a matter of lineage. Neither his father nor his grandfather were medicine men. "All I know," he says, "my parents knew I was going to be a medicine man seven months before I was born. So somebody else had to have a hand in that some way or another. If you can guess that, you'll do all right."

His family believed he had been chosen by the Great Spirit, so from the beginning he was groomed to become a medicine man. As a small child, he would go with his grandfather and uncles to the woods where they taught him the plants and their many uses as medicines. But medicines were not always required. "When I

198

was small, see eight years on up till I got about 15 years old, I doc-
tored people for toothaches, earaches, such as that, without any
medicine. I used my hand. When I was about 20 years old, I
reckon, I found out I could stop blood. You know, if people were
bleeding real bad. And I did that with my hand."

In his 20s, he went off to school in New England to learn more
about plants and their uses. He stayed for six years, and when he
returned, ailing people came to him, as they had before, and his
reputation began to spread.

He spent a lot of time leading a pony over the mountains, scour-
ing them for the many plants that he used in making his
medicines, gathering leaves, flowers, bark, roots, fruits and
stalks. "I've been all over these mountains when I was a young
fellow. I knew where these herbs were." Now, however, he hires
two men to do his foraging for him. "That's too much walk for
me. I can't climb hills like I used to," he says.

He still does the drying and mixing himself, though, here at his
trailer. "I got 634 varieties of herbs I use in making my
medicine," he says.

He needs them all. Every ailment requires a different mixture,
and the people who come seeking his help suffer from a wide
variety of ills. "Ulcerated stomach, skin troubles, gall bladder,
kidney, nervous spells, high blood," he says, reciting only a few
of those he deals with regularly. "Most of the people who come to
me are bothered with this arthritis, neuritis. I sell 'em the herbs
and they make the medicine for themselves."

Indians who live on the reservation now get free medical care
from the government, so few of them make their way to the
medicine man's hut, preferring the more modern-style medicines
dispensed without charge from the government pharmacy.
Amoneeta Sequoyah is understanding about this. "That would be
foolish for a fellow to come up here and spend his money on me,"
he says.

The demand for his herbs from others remains high, however.
"I have a lot of people. I had some people come here all the way
from New Jersey the other day. I have people come all the way
up here from Texas. I get mail orders from California, Canada,
Australia, Germany. Right here at home I guess I doctor 2,000
people during the year." Several times a year he loads up his old
Rambler with herbs and drives down to South Carolina where he
has 86 more regular customers, whom he calls patients.

The medicine man promises no cures, but he will tell stories of
miraculous things, of people who were given up by doctors and

recovered on his herb medicines. "In my 52 years of doctoring I've only lost two patients, and I didn't lose them, they lost themselves," he says. He admits that some people are beyond his help. "You can make some of the powerfulest medicine there is to be made, and if he's a man who's already been called to rest, you can't help him." Usually, he says, he can tell immediately if someone has been called and knows it is senseless to try to interfere. Sometimes, he must receive a sign. Once, when he went to gather certain herbs needed to treat a particular person, he saw the leaves of the plant wither before his touch. Then he knew.

"They is a lot of things I'd like to tell," he says, "but half the people wouldn't believe it. They'd say I was goofy or something, say I was talking out of my head, crazy talk. But I've experienced what I know, what I talk about."

Amoneeta Sequoyah says he has never been sick himself. The only time he ever was in a hospital was when a log rolled on him in the woods and broke his leg. He never gets the free medicines offered by the government.

He stands, opens the refrigerator and removes a mayonnaise jar filled with black liquid.

"That's all I take," he says, offering the jar to me. I sniff the stuff, then taste it. It is bitter but not unpleasant. "What's it for?" I ask.

"Most anything that's ailing you. There's 11 herbs in it. I take a tablespoonful twice a day. Some people come here, you know, they might be bothered by indigestion, so I give 'em a dose of this and they'll be better in about five minutes."

He begins to tell about doctors who have come to him seeking secret recipes and cures, telling him he could make big money, but he won't reveal them, won't sell them. Does he plan, I ask, to pass along his secrets before he dies? "I can't pass it along. They can't learn it. You can't learn it. It's a gift."

August, 1975
Cherokee, North Carolina

Luemer and Della Plumley
Waiting for the Power

She had thought this would be the day, and all morning Luemer Plumley, whom her sisters call Dooty, sat on the porch watching and waiting.

She watched expectantly as the power company truck lurched up the rough mountain road and one of the men got out and climbed the pole by the road and tinkered with the wires at the top, and she watched as they went on up to the church and passed back down again. And still she waited, but they didn't return.

It was almost two o'clock in the afternoon when she finally broke her silence and spoke to her sister, Della. "Deller, I just as well cook us some dinner," she said. "We're not a-goina git no power today."

"Well, Dooty," said Della, "is that what you wuz a-waitin' fer?"

With that, Luemer went into the rickety house and fired up the big wood cookstove in the tiny kitchen. She had dreaded it. This was a hot August day and the heat in the kitchen was soon almost unbearable. On a similar day a couple of weeks earlier, the preacher had come to visit and found Luemer cooking dinner. She looked at him and said, "If Hell's any hotter than this little kitchen, I sure don't want to go there, do you?"

Besides, she had been looking forward to using her new stove. It wasn't a new stove actually, just a small, used electric range. It sat in the corner across from the wood stove, plugged up and ready, but powerless. Now Luemer would have to wait for another day to use it. She guessed she could wait all right. After all, she had been waiting a good part of her life for electricity to come up Glassy Mountain.

"Been a-lookin' to git it up here fer 25 years and it didn't come," she said, "just till we got so old we couldn't enjoy it."

Glassy Mountain is in an area of Greenville County known as the Dark Corner, once a notorious moonshining district near the North Carolina border. It had always been sparsely settled, mainly by Plumleys and was one of the last mountain enclaves where electricity had not reached.

The poles came now, marching up the new road, a long, winding, unpaved gash in the mountain. This road was so steep and dangerous some mountain people refused to use it and still drove the old road, rutted and narrow, on the other side of the mountain. But others came up the new road, people from towns and cities far distant. They came in cars and trucks and jeeps, and some of them came carrying strange contraptions, great wings that they strapped to themselves so that they could leap off the cliffs at the top of the mountain and glide to landings on Highway 11, far below.

Back in the winter a jeep had come, filled with whooping people, sliding and spinning in the snow, pulling a sled wildly behind, and just in front of the house, a man had come flying head-over-heels out of the jeep and landed with a sickening thud on the bank in front of the house. The jeep went on and left him, and Luemer and Della watched, terrified, from behind the door as he struggled, cursing, in the ditch. "Every time he'd git up, he'd take the longest pause you've ever seen," Luemer would say, recalling the scene, "then he'd go back down again."

Finally, the jeep returned, and the occupants got out and snatched up the man and strapped him across the hood, tied like a trophy deer, and then the jeep careened off down the mountain. The next morning, when Luemer listened to the news on the battery radio and heard a man had been found murdered in a ditch, she was sure it was that man she had watched struggling in the ditch in front of her house.

Such goings-on the sisters had never seen before, but they were becoming a regular thing since the new road had come. "All the time," Luemer said. "It's a sight. It's awful." It had caused her to start keeping a gun close at hand. "No sir, they better not git off that road out there," she said. "I'm not a-goina fool with them ol' drunkards."

For most of their lives, the sisters' isolation on Glassy Mountain had rarely been broken. There were only three of them now. There had been four until April, when Ellen, the youngest, the talkative one, died in a hospital. Mattie, too, had been in the hospital recently. The eldest at 78, she was now living with her son off the mountain.

Only Della, 75, and Luemer, 67, remained at the old homeplace. Of the two, only Luemer had never left. Della had married and gone off down the mountain for 21 years until her husband died· in 1957, when she returned. Luemer never saw any reason for marrying or leaving the mountain.

There had been 10 of them — five boys and five girls — when they moved to this house in 1919 from another house on the mountain. It was an old house even then, built around a log cabin. Their father died the year after they moved in, and through the years the sisters watched the others go one by one. Their mother died in the house in 1946. "She laid and prayed all the time for her grandchildren to come home from the Army," Luemer said, "and just as soon as the last one come home, she died."

In all those years, neither the house nor the sisters' way of living had changed very much. They still cooked on the woodstove, fetched water from the spring, read by the light of oil lamps, plowed their garden with the help of a mule. Chickens and guinea hens scratched in the bare front yard as they always had, and hounds still lounged under the front porch. Luemer would allow no cats in the house, no dogs on the porch.

But then the new road came, bringing people and trouble from distant places, and finally the electric lines had followed (although not until the sisters and their nephew down the road and the little church up the hill had paid $1,500 each to the electric cooperative), and now Luemer knew things would never again be the same on Glassy Mountain. She had already heard that people from Greenville were coming to build vacation homes nearby.

Even after Luemer and Della had paid the money to bring the electric lines to their house, it looked for a while as if they might not get electricity after all. The house had to be wired. An electrician showed up one day and told Luemer it would cost $2,000 to do the job, but the sisters had no money left. Then Jim Tankersley, a former revenuer, heard about it. He'd known the Plumley sisters for many years, and he came up the mountain one day with a friend from Greenville, Shorty Vaughn, and they wired the house at no charge. Not long afterward, Shorty came back bringing the electric range.

"He said he'd fotch a Kelvinator next Sunday or the next," Luemer said. "I wouldn't've had lights at all if it wouldn't've been for keepin' milk. I told 'em all along I didn't care about power. But we love our milk and butter, and you can't keep it in this heat."

Luemer didn't know what the hold-up was about getting the power on. She'd thought the men might come back after dinner, but a storm came instead. It brought sharp lightning and heavy black clouds that sent water gushing down the gullies in the road, "a real field soaker," Luemer called it.

When the storm had passed, Luemer and Della sat on the porch with visitors, enjoying the freshness and coolness the rain had brought. Luemer told about lying in wait in the chickenhouse for a blacksnake that was stealing her eggs and finding nine unbroken eggs inside it when she killed it. Della, a thin, frail woman, told how she swelled so bad and never felt good anymore and had to go to bed before dark every day.

The subject of television came up. Luemer laughed when she was asked if she'd ever watched TV. "I've not watched one enough for my head to stop swimmin'. Only time I ever watched one was Billy Graham, that big preacher, and ever' time I was about to git interested, they cut 'im off."

"Would you watch it if you had one?" I asked.

"I guess everybody does, I would too."

Two chickens got into a dispute over something one of them had scratched up in the yard. The dogs came out from under the porch, where Della had shooed them, and loped off toward the road. "They goin' now to hunt a squirrel," Della said. Somebody mentioned how nice and cool and quiet it was on the mountain now, and Luemer looked at the electric lines that still dangled, unconnected, on the side of the house and said she expected surely the men would come tomorrow and cut on the power so she wouldn't have to put up with that hot kitchen again.

August, 1978
Glassy Mountain, South Carolina

Tank Tankersley
Revenuer

"You're in the middle of likker territory right here," Jim
Tankersley said. "Everything you see, I've walked. I've cut stills
all along here."

We were driving along Highway 11 in the mountainous area of
Greenville County known as the Dark Corner, near the North
Carolina line. At one time, the Dark Corner was notorious as a
moonshine whiskey center, one of the nation's leading areas of
production. For 25 years, Jim Tankersley was the man who
chased the moonshiners. They called him Tank, and he is now a
legend in the area.

Tank laughed and pointed out a small house alongside a creek.
"Ol' Richard there, I caught 'im up in that little creek, came right
back, caught 'im again the next Christmas. Same place. Some of
'em told 'im, said, 'Ol' Tank's goina send you to the penitentiary,'
and he said, 'Ol' Tank wouldn't take a thousand dollars fer me.
I'm too easy kotched.' "

Until his retirement in 1977, Tank was an agent of the Federal
Bureau of Alcohol, Tobacco and Firearms — a "revenooer." He
was a good one. He probably destroyed as many stills, poured out
as much mash, caught as many moonshiners, confiscated as
much liquor and as many liquor-running cars as any officer ever
did. "We have cut 12 or 13 stills a day," he was saying. "I made a
lot of cases. I worked reckless. I'd take my chances. I was fast, and
I could run." Running was important. "Oh, yeah. Yes sir. You
caught 'em. They didn't wait for you. Yes sir, you had to run and
run hard."

Tank had always kept in good shape. He had been born in this
area, had prowled the mountains with his father, a game
warden, had played football in high school before going off to
combat in World War II. After the war, he returned home and
went to work for the highway patrol. He soon took a job as a
sheriff's deputy assigned to sniffing out moonshiners in the area
where he had grown up. He proved so good at it that he was
hired as a federal agent in 1952 when moonshining was at its
peak.

"Back in those days there wasn't many people around here

who sometime or another hadn't had to fool with a little whiskey. Hard times, you know. It was hard to make a living up here. Farming just wouldn't do. So as a way of life, they made a little illegal likker. It was a big thing."

Legend had the mountain moonshiners growing a little corn and turning it into whiskey in copper stills. But the moonshiners rarely used copper stills, said Tank. Copper was too expensive and it got too hot and burned the mash. And the whiskey that was made was almost exclusively "sugar likker," made with sugar, yeast and "shorts," the remains of wheat after millers are finished with it, usually sold as feed for hogs. "There never was a whole lot of corn likker," Tank said. "They's a few people around who know how to make it, but I guess 90 per cent of 'em didn't even know how to make corn. Corn likker's a slow process. It takes a lot of time, puts you out there in the woods too long. More work in it. It's slow runnin'. You can't hurry it. You can't push it. If you do, it'll burn. You'll hear a few oldtimers say, 'Boy, I'd give anything for a pint of pure corn likker. They's people'll argue with you that pure corn likker tastes better than sugar likker. But it's got oil in it. Unless you strain that oil out, it'll give you a headache. 'Course if you drink enough of *any* of it, it'll give you a headache."

Tank had known some of the moonshiners he chased, but they never resented his efforts to catch them, he said. "See, I was just on the opposite side and they knew that. They respected that. They'd cuss and snort and raise the devil sometimes, but that was about all it ever amounted to. They didn't get too hostile about it. Ninety per cent of the time, I didn't have a gun and they knew it. You'd hardly ever go into a still where you didn't know somebody."

There was a sort of code of honor between revenuer and moonshiner. If Tank chased and caught them, they rarely resisted. If he didn't catch them, but knew who they were, he didn't go back after them later but waited for another time to catch them in the act. At times, when he ran into barbed wire fences in the night, or fell and hurt himself during the chase, the moonshiners would come back and help him. "They was the first ones to help you when you got in trouble. Ninety per cent of 'em was good people. When they told you something, you could count on 'em doing it."

When Tank was seriously injured in a car wreck while chasing a moonshine runner near Greenville, the halls of the hospital filled with moonshiners who came to pay their respects and offer assistance to his family. When the moonshiners got into trouble, they frequently turned to Tank, who oftentimes was the man who had caused their problems. "You'd try to get 'em in jail, you know," he said, chuckling, "and then try to get 'em out. Feel sorry for 'em, go down and talk to the judge."

Nowadays, Tank sees mostly ex-moonshiners as he rides the back roads of the mountains, and they wave to him and stop to chat. Some of them still come to him when they have problems, and they know they can always depend on him to do what he can to help. Moonshining continued fairly strong into the '60s, Tank was saying, but by the early '70s, he could see that it was almost over. In his last few years as an agent, he was more and more often being sent on special assignments that had nothing to do with moonshining. When he prowled the mountains, he was as apt to find a marijuana field (usually planted by a city dweller) as a still. After his retirement at age 56, no new revenuer was assigned to search out stills in the Dark Corner. He was the last one. "Last word I got they wasn't even foolin' with illegal likker anymore," he said. "It's over now. Oh, there's still a few stills around, but I guess it's more than 90 per cent gone. One of the things that hurt white likker most was prosperity. It wasn't anything not so long ago to find a man with a pint of white likker in his car or his house. But as prosperity came on, they got ashamed of that. You had to have red likker, store-bought likker. You'd talk to 'em out in public and they'd say, 'Oh, I wouldn't drink that stuff at all, that white likker. That stuff'll kill you.' But the lead poisoning wasn't that bad when the likker was made in the mountains. That was just scare stuff."

For a while he drove without saying anything, then he laughed and started telling about an old moonshiner named Bill. "Ol' Bill, we caught 'im so much it got to where it wasn't even fun to catch 'im. But ol' Bill, law, he was a character. He was a legend . . ."

September, 1978
River Falls, South Carolina